Young Offenders

Young Offenders

LORD LONGFORD

Chapmans

Chapmans Publishers
A division of The Orion Publishing Group Ltd
Orion House
5 Upper St Martin's Lane
London WC2H 9EA

First published by Chapmans 1993

*A CIP catalogue record for this book is available from the
British Library*

ISBN 1–85592–653–9

*Photoset in Monophoto Galliard by
Selwood Systems, Midsomer Norton
Printed and bound in Great Britain by
Butler & Tanner Ltd,
Frome and London*

To Elizabeth

Acknowledgments

So many people have helped me to write this book, many of them giving up much of their time, that I cannot begin to thank them enough. I hope that those who are quoted in the pages that follow will feel that some small justice has been done them.

Within my personal circle, my thanks go in the first place to Gwen Keeble, my intimate colleague of many years; to Barbara Winch who, with her husband Peter, has helped my family in so many ways; to Kitty Chapman with her kindly presence; to the ever efficient staff of the Susan Hamilton Secretariat (Westminster), whether under Jane or her successor Elizabeth; and to Matthew Oliver, sternest of critics.

Elizabeth has spared time from her more exalted duties to help me at every moment.

Contents

Prelude

The House of Commons, 2 March 1993

On 2 March 1993, Mr Kenneth Clarke, the Home Secretary, announced an important new initiative in regard to young offenders. The main feature was the proposed establishment of a small number – possibly five – of secure units for young offenders aged 12, 13, 14 and 15, with up to 40 offenders in each unit. This proposal was part of a wider scheme to increase discipline in schools and children's homes through the agency of the Department of Education and the Department of Health.

The proposals were immediately denounced by the leading penal reform and children's organizations. There was, indeed, widespread criticism in serious quarters. The heading of a leading article in *The Times* was typical: 'Panic Over Crime: the government's new policy has been hastily conceived.' *The Times* recognized recent public alarm over the murder of a 2-year-old boy, allegedly by two boys of 10 and 11. In addition, a judge had decided (his decision was later overruled) not to send a 15-year-old rapist into protective custody, and soon after Mr Clarke's statement a schoolteacher was raped by a boy of 13 with the assistance of a boy of 14. *The Times* noted that 'One horrific child murder does not make a crime wave', and went on to point out that Mr Clarke's initiative could only be justified if the initiative, carefully thought through, had been held ready in the Home Office for just such a moment. 'Yesterday's statement on juvenile crime did not meet that test,' *The Times* continued. 'It had all the hallmarks of a policy both conceived and announced in panic ... The best thing Mr Clarke can now do is cast about for ideas from

1

the public, voluntary and private sectors for the type of regime the schools should offer.'

This book was sent to press at the time of Mr Clarke's pronouncement. His latest proposals are considered in my concluding chapter together with other views he has expressed publicly or to me in writing. It should be mentioned here that the Lord Chief Justice has recently expressed dissatisfaction with the 1991 Criminal Justice Act, and an urgent inquiry into the workings of the Act has been ordered by the Home Secretary. A good deal must be expected on the subject before this book is published.

When Harold Wilson formed his Cabinet in 1964, I entered it as Leader of the House of Lords. My friend the late Evelyn Waugh wrote to another friend, Lady Donaldson, that he was so glad that I was not to be Home Secretary, 'Otherwise we should have all been murdered in our beds'. It may be that such a comment might be heard today, if the appointment in question existed on this side of fantasy. I hope, however, that readers will feel that the views of the Home Secretary and the police have not been neglected in what follows. They carry a heavy responsibility for our safety, while penal reformers will never cease to press for more enlightened treatment for offenders young and old.

Covent Garden, 8 May 1992

Called at New Horizon Youth Centre, founded by myself and others in 1968. Interviewed three young people selected by Peter, the Director: Peter, aged 21, Stephen, aged 22, June, aged 20. Peter and Stephen are healthy, over 6 ft tall; June, quite small, is definitely pretty. None of them, it was clear, had considered policy matters or asked themselves how they could have been treated differently. All, for one reason or another, had parted from their families and were sleeping rough. All seemed to prefer such a way of life to any kind of hostel (June said that she loved it) because of the regulations there. All, however, were hoping to obtain their own flats before long. All had been in trouble with the law – Peter and Stephen repeatedly. Peter for thieving, which did not seem to have landed him in prison; Stephen for possession of an offensive weapon – which did. He told me that a knife was an essential defence if one was sleeping rough. He had, however, abandoned the knife and recently was badly cut on the lower arm by a gang who considered him an intruder.

June told me a story that I still find hard to credit. She said that she and a friend were walking about near Victoria at 9 p.m. one night when they were arrested by police. Net result: she got six months for assaulting the police. Very hard to credit.

All three represent the homeless, sleeping rough, who live on the edge of crime. None of them had valuable comments on the penal system, but Stephen seemed to have made some good friends there. All of them seemed reluctant to obtain income support, even when it was available. One of them told me that it was positively dangerous, because other beggars gathered round the office and were liable to steal the money received. I pointed out the problem of people like myself when confronted by a well-grown young beggar. They said in effect that that was their problem.

Lambeth, 19 May 1992

Entertained a party from the North Lambeth Intermediate Treatment Centre. None of the young people attending is sent by the courts. They are of school age and proved impossible to teach in the State schools.

The NLITC provides full-time education, the young people continuing to live at home. In fact, four young people were brought to tea, three girls and a boy. One of the girls told me she was excluded from school because engaged in so many fights. The other two described themselves as getting on very badly with their families, although they continued to live at home. The young man had been convicted of robbery with violence, the violence consisting of a replica gun.

Westminster, 20 May 1992

Gave tea to an assistant manager of the St Charles Youth Treatment Centre in Brentwood. He brought along two boys, one aged 18, one 16. The 18-year-old boy was the son of a Professor of Mathematics. He was 6 ft 2 in tall and very good-looking. He had been convicted of robbery and indecent assault and given three years. He would be leaving St Charles shortly and hoped to qualify for university. He told me, 'I have been privileged to be at St Charles.' I did not pursue the economics of St Charles on this occasion, but when I visited it a little while ago I was told that it cost £100,000 a year to keep someone there. They have 90 staff looking after 30 inmates. I am reminded sadly of the old Barlinnie Special Unit in Glasgow, where 16 staff were looking after 4 inmates.

The other young man provided a sharp contrast of background. His father is serving a ten-year sentence for sexual assault. He himself, having been sexually assaulted by his father, did the same to his younger brother and sisters. He was placed in care. Aged 16,

3

he hopes and expects to remain in care for some time. He wants to become a hairdresser and is at present working as a trainee outside the centre.

The House of Lords, 24 June 1992

'I want to mention a case referred to by Judge Tumim, the Chief Inspector of Prisons, in the interim report on the young offender institution remand centre at Feltham. ... The preface records that Her Majesty's Coroner to Surrey had just written to the judge following the inquest he had held on a boy of 15 who hanged himself recently at Feltham. Judge Tumim explained that the coroner made two points that he would report and endorse. First, the boy was sentenced to 188 days by magistrates in Norfolk. That is about 200 miles from Feltham, which was nevertheless the nearest available place for him. He received no family visits as a result. When a relative died he was too far away to attend the funeral. Then, at weekends, a juvenile, he had only two periods of daily association, one hour in the morning and two hours in the afternoon. From 4.30 p.m. each day he was locked up and isolated for some 16 hours. That was the way we treated a child of 15 in Britain in 1991. In my view it represents a truly scandalous situation.' Lord Harris of Greenwich, in the debate on young offenders which I initiated on 14 June 1992.

'I believe profoundly that programmes of activities in which young people are encouraged or required to take part under supervision should be introduced, with the accent on their usefulness rather than punishment. The more that young offenders are enabled to take part, along with non-offending groups, and can become integrated into the local community without being labelled offenders, the more they are likely to abandon crime and change for the better.' Lord Hunt of Llanfair Waterdine.

'I believe that young offender institutions should themselves be phased out and eventually closed. Even in the best of them young offenders have a 70 per cent or higher rate of return to crime after two years from the date of their release.' Lord Henderson of Brompton.

'We expect courts to make greater use of community sentences than they have in the past.' Lord Astor, for the government.

'Does the Noble Lord realize that the Inspector's latest criticisms [of Feltham Young Offenders' Institution] are based on anxieties expressed by the governor and his staff?' Lord Longford.

'I pay tribute to the imaginative way in which the governor has employed his staff.' Lord Astor, for the government.

I pressed the government strongly to accept the demand by

NACRO that offenders aged 15 should no longer be sent to prison. The most interesting question, I said, is this: If there is to be change, what is to be done with those young people who now go into penal custody? Where else do you send them?

'Secure accommodation is a specialized resource which takes a long time to plan and build.' Lord Astor, for the government.

He was unable to indicate, even vaguely, whether any extra resources would be forthcoming.

Deeds are better than words but words are better than nothing.

Brighton, 7 October 1992

Through the courtesy of the *Catholic Herald*, I am enabled to visit the Gorgon in her lair. I am sitting in the front row of seats reserved for journalists at the Conservative Party Conference. The Home Secretary is speaking. One sentence only do I quote at this point in the book: 'It is young offenders who are causing the problems which are the most difficult to solve.'

Introduction

I inherited my interest in the cause of youth from my uncle, my mother's brother, Arthur Villiers, second son of the Earl of Jersey. He was a successful merchant banker (Baring Brothers), but his influence on me was far removed from that. For over 50 years, apart from the First World War in which he won a DSO and bar, he lived in Hackney Wick, East London, presiding over the Eton Manor Club, the largest boys' club in London.

I spent endless nights there, before I married, and kept in touch afterwards. I took part in all the sporting activities, playing in their first rugger match and going to annual camp. I cannot measure efficiently the long-term effect of my uncle's life at Eton Manor. He always said that sport broke down the barrier between the classes as nothing else could. No one ever talked about crime in my hearing. Looking back, I suppose that some of the boys (13–18 year-olds) must have got into trouble with the law. But it never occurred to me at the time.

I became a prison visitor in Oxford in the 1930s. In the middle 1950s I became very active in that area, conducting an inquiry for the Nuffield Foundation into the causes of crime, opening the first debate in the House of Lords on prisons, and founding, with others, the New Bridge for Ex-Prisoners. My interest in youth work did not flag. I initiated the first debate in the Lords on the Youth Service; in 1964, I not only started the first debate in the Lords on victims of crime but was also chairman of a Labour Party committee which produced a seminal report on the treatment of crimes. However, it was Baroness Serota, when she was chairman of the Children's Committee of the LCC, who really brought home to me the need to keep children and adolescents out of prison.

In 1968, I resigned from the Labour Cabinet because of the failure to keep their promise to raise the school-leaving age to 16. Strong in my desire to do something for young people, I initiated, with others, the New Horizon Youth Centre. I had originally envisaged it as intended for young delinquents, but I was quickly persuaded to throw it open to all the young between 16 and 21. Today, they employ a dozen social workers receiving 3,000 homeless young people a year.

In the last 21 years I have taken part in a great number of debates on penal matters in the house of Lords, initiating many of them. In 1991, I published *Punishment and the Punished* on adults offenders and in 1992 *Prisoner or Patient*, which dealt with the treatment of mentally disordered offenders. It will be quickly noticed that young offenders have not hitherto received a proper measure of attention from me. This book is an attempt to rectify that omission.

How far should the principles applicable to adults apply to those under 21, particularly to those who can only be described as children? Many views will be expressed in the following pages on this and the wider issues affecting the behaviour of our young people. My conclusions will be offered at the end.

The Facts of Crime

The facts about the extent of crime by young offenders are not, as will be seen in a moment, as simple as one could wish. Lord Astor, a Minister at the Home Office, said with legitimate pride in June 1992 that, 'The number of juveniles under 17 years of age sentenced to custody fell from about 8,000 in 1981 to about 1,600 in 1990. For young adults aged 17–20 the use of custodial sentences fell from about 21,500 to 13,300 in over the same period. Using a slightly different basis of calculation, there were 10,500 under 21 in custody in 1980 and only 6,400 in 1990.' So far, so good.

But when one tries to measure the extent of crime by young offenders over the decade, one runs into difficulties. I studied carefully the helpful figures on page 127 of *Criminal Statistics 1990*, published by the Home Office. One begins with figures which refer to persons found guilty at all courts for indictable offences. The total number of persons found guilty or cautioned in this way dropped from 555,000 to 509,000 between 1980 and 1990; the figure was 518,000 in 1991. It is difficult to square these figures with the information provided on page 23 of the latest (1991) edition of *Criminal Statistics:*

The number of notifiable offences recorded by the police has increased from 3.0 million in 1981 to 5.3 million in 1991: on average about 6 per cent each year. Of this 2.3 million increase, about 2.2 million were offences against property ... although crimes of violence (i.e. violence against the person, sexual offences and robbery) increased at a faster rate.

Over a longer period recorded crime has risen nine-fold since 1950. The rate per 100,000 population ... increased from about 1,100 in 1950 to just over 10,000 in 1991. The average annual percentage increase over the past 40 years was about 5.7 per cent. The rate was higher in the earlier

8

period 1950–70 (6.1 per cent) than in the later period 1970–1990 (5.2 per cent).

I raised the 1990 figures with the statistical department of the Home Office, the highest authority in such a matter. They took great trouble to be helpful but would not claim, I think, that they cleared up what I still regard as a mystery. I had better give their actual words:

As you suggest, the picture is a little different if summary and indictable offences are taken together. The bottom row of Table 1.1 of *Criminal Statistics* shows an increase in total number of offenders dealt with. The top row of that Table also shows that the *number* of offences cleared up by the police has increased. However, the *rate* of increase in clear-ups is lower (38 per cent) than the rate of increase in offences (69 per cent), which means that the gap widens. Another part of the explanation may be an increase in the use of informal methods of dealing with alleged offenders which do not get into the clear-up figures. This is largely speculation since we do not collect centrally information about informal action. But my speculation is not helpful to you, nor any more soundly based than your own.

Let that pass for the moment. There is no doubt on the figures provided that compared with adults the proportion of young people found guilty or cautioned declined quite noticeably over the period. In 1980, persons under 21 found guilty or cautioned were 54 per cent of the total. By 1990, the proportion had dropped to 46 per cent. These figures would appear to provide good ammunition for writers like Professor Andrew Rutherford and others who are anxious to prove that the more enlightened sentencing policy adopted during this period has gone hand in hand with a decline in young offending. In spite of his enthusiasm, Andrew Rutherford is careful not to state a dogmatic conclusion. Here again it seems best to quote the exact words of the Home Office.

You ask next about changes in youth crime. The first point I must make is that we do not have any accurate measure of youth crime. We do not know the ages of those who committed offences which were not cleared up. The best measure we have is the number of known offenders (i.e., those cautioned or convicted), but, as you point out, this is an imprecise guide. Demographic changes might account for part of the decline in the overall number of known young offenders. Table 5.25 of *Criminal Statistics* shows that there were fewer people aged 10 to 20 in the population in 1990 than in 1980. A somewhat better guide is the numbers of known offenders per 100,000 population. You will find the figures (for indictable offences) at the bottom of Table 5.22. These confirm the decline for 10–16 year-olds, but show an increase for the 17–20 age group. Again, a possible increase in the use of informal disposals may also have contributed to the drop in the number of known offenders.

The Home Office expert goes on to deal with a question from me about 'the relationship between changes in methods of dealing with young people and changes in recorded offences'. Here, once again, he remains inflexible in resisting what he calls 'speculation': 'I am afraid that I am not prepared to speculate whether the more lenient approach for young people led to a reduction in youth crime.' Nevertheless, on the face of it, Andrew Rutherford and those who think like him have an attractive case.

We can at least conclude that the more lenient sentencing of the past decade has not led to a proportionate increase of crime among young people. While this book was going to press, new figures regarding crime and the prison population continued to pour out. In my view and that of the experts I have spoken to these new figures do not invalidate my conclusions here.

The Causes of Young Offending

It is difficult, even impossible, to separate the causes of crime in general from the causes of young offending. My original mandate, when I undertook an inquiry in the 1950s for the Nuffield Foundation, was to look into the causes of juvenile crime, but by common consent we moved into the ones of crime in general. I was assisted by a particularly strong group of experts and between us the existing information was thoroughly combed, with the help of expert witnesses.

At the end of the inquiry, I gave this very limited account of our contribution: 'I feel we have made very little progress in recent years in distinguishing and assessing the strength of the factors responsible for our national volume of crime. I feel, however, that we have made very considerable, but still limited, progress in deciding what causes have tended to make any particular man a criminal.' I found pleasure in something of perhaps even greater importance: 'I find it possible to be more encouraging about one direction in which substantial progress has been made by the criminologists in recent years. I feel that our whole approach to crime and to the criminal has been very much altered for the better.'

On one aspect of the subject, I was prepared to be a little more definite:

We have become vastly more aware:

1. Of the statistical connection between homes broken in the physical sense and crime of all kinds.

2. Of the possibly lasting damage inflicted by the separation of a small child from his mother.

3. Of the possibly lasting damage inflicted by the lack of mother love during

11

the first few years, even where the home is intact and the child remains with his mother.

4. Of the need for security as an element of healthy growth in the perfect home.

Well, that is how I left it after all that expert help, in the mid-1950s, and so far as I recollect my standpoint was not denounced by critics.

Since then, there has been voluminous writing about the causes of crime and, more particularly, juvenile crime. As I hinted earlier, I cannot think that any government today has been given any guidance much more positive as a consequence. This is not to disparage a better understanding of the individual criminal, as I said 35 years ago. Many good judges would, I think, treat *The Delinquent Way of Life* by Professor D. J. West and David Farrington as the nearest thing to a classic that has appeared on the subject. The book was published in 1977. Their book was the third report on a project called *The Cambridge Study of Delinquent Development*, which followed up the lives of some 400 boys born between 1951 and 1954. Near the end, West and Farrington write: 'Our previous work demonstrated that a constellation of adverse factors present at an early age, notably large families, low intelligence, poverty, unsatisfactory parental child-rearing behaviour, and parental criminology, increase very significantly the likelihood of a boy acquiring a juvenile delinquency record.'

By far the most important conclusion is spelt out with much eloquence in the final chapter: 'Official thinking proclaims that measures applied to juvenile offenders are primarily intended to help rather than to exact retribution.' West and Farrington state emphatically that, in practice, 'they prove harmful', and they continue: 'For all these reasons, we should like to see appropriate welfare intervention applied as far as possible outside the context of criminal convictions and the criminal justice system.' Help received voluntarily from health and welfare agencies would be more acceptable and might prove more effective than a direct attack upon delinquent habits by agents of the criminal courts. Without going into more detail about the kind of preventive action that might be taken before the individual has become a confirmed social misfit, they mention, in particular, schools and youth centres as places where a constructive influence could be exerted. They mention job training, counselling in the roles of parenthood, advice on household budgeting and management, even coaching in civic rights and responsibilities. But by and large the message is the one that has been adopted with

12

such success in the 1980s of keeping young people out of custody wherever possible.

West and Farrington may fairly claim to have given a powerful thrust in that direction. What they did not address, however, is this: when young offenders have to be placed under restraint but penal custody is to be avoided, what secure arrangements should be made for them as an alternative? I hope that the following pages will provide some answers.

Feltham Young Offenders' Institution

Feltham Young Offenders' Institution was severely censured in 1992 by Judge Stephen Tumim, Her Majesty's Chief Inspector of Prisons.

I have gone at some length into the tragic story of one inmate, Lee Waite, who committed suicide in Feltham, and his mother Pauline Waite. But that tragic story should be considered as part of the events which have brought down such severe criticism on Feltham. It cannot be dissociated from the noble efforts being made by the Governor and many of its staff to bring about a radical improvement.

I met Pauline Waite for the first time when she spoke at an Open Day at Feltham. On this well-attended occasion, a Friends of Feltham Society was founded. It was remarkable enough that Mrs Waite should have been asked to speak. What followed was more remarkable still. At the request of the Governor, she opened a new wing, named after her son, which was intended to house trouble-makers, more particularly the kind of bullies who had driven her son to death. Later, she came to lunch with me and was interviewed at the House of Lords.

The conclusion of her own speech was in complete harmony with the aspirations of the very experienced and idealistic Governor, Joe Whitty. She called for Feltham's inmates to have full and proper education, more time out of their cells, and more meaningful activities during the day. It was impossible not to sympathize with her final words: 'The system killed my son.'

Nothing could have been blunter at the inquest into Lee's death than the Governor's criticisms of the present situation in his prison. He came back again and again, as he has done many times since in

14

defiance of government inertia, to the need for perhaps 40 more staff:

There is a lack of staff; there is a lack of facilities and there is a lack of meaningful activities. We are short of staff to produce people at the courts. I have to withdraw staff from other resources for them to go to the courts. ... If there is a lack of activity, you get bullying. ... If the inmates are not occupied, they create terror. It is the Feltham threat. I know it.

When asked about surveillance, Governor Whitty replied: 'If there were proper supervision, there would be less likelihood of injuries.' But once again shortage of staff makes adequate supervision impossible. It is not difficult, in the light of these and other similar comments, to summarize his argument: shortage of staff means lack of supervision and lack of activities, hence what can only be described as terror.

It is noteworthy that Governor Whitty considered that in his criticisms of Feltham the Chief Inspector of Prisons 'came down the wrong road when seeing it in psychiatric terms'. He refers to his charges as 'problem kids', but 'they don't need doctors'. What they do need are activities: 'They don't even have table tennis.' The Governor did not confine himself to administration issues.

It is no part of my task to apportion praise or blame to the staff of Feltham who theoretically might have prevented these suicides. What does come out of the evidence is that a high proportion of the youths entering Feltham have talked of suicide at some time or other. They cannot all be put in a hospital. It should be emphasized that since the death of Lee Waite and three other boys there, cameras have been introduced to enable staff to pick out the bullies, and a special wing, as mentioned above, has been opened for them and other trouble-makers.

I interviewed Mrs Pauline Waite, Lee's mother, on 22 July 1992. What follows is her story of life in Feltham.

LORD LONGFORD: It is rather extraordinary that these young people in Feltham are locked up each day for such long period. The Governor is convinced that he should have more staff. Do you think that is the answer?

PAULINE WAITE: I think that is part of the answer – they definitely do need more staff. After my second visit, I thought that some of the staff had a very old-fashioned attitude. I spoke to one who said that there was no bullying at Feltham. He said that a few months previously, the word 'bullying' had been used. The press got hold of it and it had somehow stuck. 'I have no bullying on my wing,' he said. 'I respect them and they respect me.' His was one of the smaller units and things could well have been so. In the Quail Wing, where Lee had been held, numbers were much larger. When they had association, there were only 2 officers to 30 boys. If my son had seen a therapist we might have learnt what the problem was. You would think that he needed some sort of constructive therapy.

LL: Some sort of positive therapy?

PW: It could be made an option. At the moment what option has the magistrate got? There is only release on bail or Feltham. If we could have a third option – therapy.

LL: One does feel that Lee needed some sort of therapeutic treatment. At Fairbridge in North Lambeth, in the experimental unit, the lads go on adventure projects.

PW: You are the only person who has put that to me. That is possibly the answer. The need to steal cars is like an addiction. It is not something that can be explained away.

LL: Did Lee have a driving licence?

PW: Yes. He was in the army for a year, until he suffered a back injury. He probably needed someone outside the family to get at the root of it all.

LL: Now, take those bullies – as you can imagine, I would like to go to Feltham and see some of them. People behave worse when they are in a gang.

PW: Some of them came from deprived areas, from homes where there is no love or any kind of upbringing. They got hold of him somehow. They tortured him and he committed suicide the same night. He was found on the 31st. The last time he was checked was on Friday night and he was still alive then. They do have security guards on duty at night. One asked him if he was all right and thought he heard a grunt. Nobody said definitely that it happened in the showers. We only learnt recently that I should have been given the opportunity of identifying the body. I was given the option of having a *post mortem*. There were marks on his body to show that he had been interfered with.

LL: You mean rape?

PW: My husband spoke to the Governor and he promised that he would get to the truth.

16

LL: Would these people have been put in the bullies' unit now?

PW: Yes, they certainly would have been.

LL: When I was there, the boys all seemed to be lying around on their beds. In remand centres they cannot be made to do anything. Do you agree with me that they should be made to do something? Of course, that would call for quite big alterations.

PW: I agree.

LL: To come back to the question of bullying – your son was badly bullied. He had been in the army and must have been able to look after himself?

PW: My opinion is that each individual is a human being able to look after himself to a certain extent. Lee was brought up on the average housing estate, but at Feltham he was up against very streetwise black thugs. He was called a 'Fraggle' in their jargon – one who did not come from London and was, moreover, white, so an obvious target.

LL: The ones who bullied your son were black?

PW: Yes. People are too much worried about what the black community are going to think or feel, but this question of prejudice works both ways.

LL: What proportion of those on remand at Feltham at that time were black?

PW: More than half. It is a big problem. Unless you come from London and are black, you are a 'Fraggle'.

LL: I had not realized that that was such a big problem there. Would you say that in Feltham this bullying was mainly a black problem?

PW: From what I have heard, and I have spoken with my son's friends who say that at Feltham the white boys who do not come from London are very frightened at the thought of being sent there. One of those I spoke to said that he would rather live in a sewer than go back there. He was much older than my son, had been in trouble several times and was very streetwise. He would do anything rather than go back there and appeared to be terrified of the place.

LL: I have associated with the black community in Brixton. They talk a good deal against discrimination. Now your son was bullied – does it hurt you too much to tell me exactly what happened?

PW: He was remanded to Feltham on Monday, 26th August 1991.

For the first few days he was with a friend. They had been picked up together for sharing a stolen car. They were brought up at Luton Magistrates' Court and the friend was sent to Glen Parva. Lee was sent back to Feltham.

LL: Was your son strong or was he rather small?

PW: He was not skinny – he was of average build, 6 feet tall. Now, a couple of days before – he and his friend having been separated – there had been an attempt to take Lee's watch away from him. There was a fight. Lee fought back and the situation calmed down. That night there was a lot of shouting going on and Lee was told that he would be sorted out in the showers and was going to die. The officers deny hearing anything of this. They do not go into the showers, but remain on duty outside. The shouting went on when they were locked up at night. On the Friday – probably in the late afternoon –Lee was assaulted. There were five of them – we don't know if all of them set about him. One of the boys saw them talking to Lee in an unfriendly way. Lee was told to take his trainers [shoes] off. They were quite new. He was given a shabby old pair in exchange. As he handed them over, his watch was snatched. The next thing we know is that, at nine o'clock that night, he was again assaulted – his injuries were so bad that he must have screamed out at the time.

LL: I would have thought that officers were present.

PW: I can't believe that no one heard anything – but it did take place in the showers.

LL: You would think that prison officers who are human beings and are professionals – you would not think that they would necessarily be lying in this case, unless they had been negligent.

PW: Nobody seems to have heard anything.

LL: You have a very good, if painful, perspective on all this. Your son got involved in stealing cars. Can you think, looking back, that there was any way of preventing it? I don't say that parents are responsible; nevertheless, earlier on, was there no way of your preventing him?

PW: I would like to think that there was something I should have done, because I would like to blame myself. I don't think people should say that the parents are to blame. You do what you think is right at the time.

LL: Did he do quite well at school?

PW: He was still at school when he stole my car. I was at work and the car was parked in the drive. I never locked it, but kept a spare ignition key hidden indoors. He had come home from school with a friend, took the car and went for a drive. They were soon followed by a police car. We only knew about it at the time because the car suffered a bit of damage. Already he had this obsession with cars. I did threaten him, but to no avail.

LL: Had he a father?

PW: No, a stepfather. His father died in 1983. Lee was charmer – he could charm the leaves off the trees. He was a nice kid – he never bullied or answered back.

LL: When he came out of the army was he employed?

PW: It revolved round cars – it always came back to cars.

LL: Do you think there is any alternative to Feltham? There is a theory that nobody under 18 should be sent to penal custody. But where do you send them?

PW: If you've got criminals, they need to be put under supervision. I think Feltham's biggest problem is its vast catchment area. On the remand side, you have 500 boys between the ages of 14 and 20, sometimes hundreds of miles away from home and family – a very volatile situation. It should be a smaller establishment and more of them. One boy was only 15 when he died there – his parents came from Yarmouth.

LL: Can you think of any other kind of place than Feltham? They do speak of supervision in the community.

PW: I think something like a children's home, but with restrictions – like a bail hostel, where they have to answer to someone. Something along those lines, but with more supervision, not necessarily reporting to a police station, but that sort of thing. I am not really sure what I am looking for. It has got to be more of a local form of supervision.

It remains to offer a few reflections on the sad life of Lee Waite. He joined the army as a boy soldier, hurt his back quite badly and was discharged as unsuitable. A passion for cars, that is to say for stealing and driving cars, took over. He left home and, not surprisingly, found himself in serious trouble. His mother naturally has asked herself many times what she or anyone could have done to prevent his arrival at Feltham. No obvious answer has presented itself. She argues convincingly that this car mania with him was an addiction like drugs or alcohol. He needed therapy, undoubtedly. But what

19

form of therapy and at what point could it have been provided?

On 30 July 1992 I paid my fourth visit to Feltham Young Offenders' Institution. This time the Governor had arranged for me to see several of the young inmates, together with the young female psychologist who, as part of the medical team, would be helping to service the special new wing for trouble-makers.

The first young man was in Albatross, referred to these days as the therapeutic wing. Before seeing him, I had very helpful conversations with the prison officers in charge. There were 20 young men with 8 officers to look after them. All had volunteered for the wing, as had the officers. The latter did not possess formal qualifications beyond their experience in the Prison Service. I understand that they may receive more training in future, but I could not help reflecting that qualified nursing officers receive six months' training. The therapy in Albatross mainly takes the form of group work. This has its own perils for the invigilating staff. One of them showed me a wrist which had been broken by a member of the group who was displeased with his intervention.

The young man in question was 21 and about to move to an adult prison. He had been in and out of penal institutions (and care) since the age of 14. He attributed much of his troubles to drugs, including heroin, which he had been using since he was 13. He was unqualified in his praise of the help given him at Albatross. For the first time, he had been able to look into himself. He felt confident that he would be able to keep away from drugs in future. I could only hope that an adult prison would continue to give him the kind of help he had received in Feltham.

I saw another seven men from Albatross. All of them praised the unit and agreed that they had benefited from it. They were not, however, uncritical, claiming a lack of activities and education. I was told later that if they had been keen on education while in Albatross they could have got it. All of them, like the first young man, had been in and out of institutions since puberty. I was left asking myself how they could have been assisted earlier to reject a life of delinquency.

One rather interesting comment was made by a tough-looking youngster who said that he thought he had improved in some ways. The self-knowledge he had acquired should keep him out of crime. But in other ways, he said, 'I have got worse. I am more selfish.' Perhaps this must be attributed to the inevitable damage done by confinement, perhaps more hopefully to the fact that he had become more aware of his existing selfishness.

I then moved on to Nightingale which I had visited on an earlier occasion. This wing has ambitious arrangements for keeping in

20

touch with the families of its inmates. I was also aware of the harmonious relations between the inmates and the staff, and that the inmates in many cases work outside. Their seven-a-side rugby team play in the Twickenham League. The inhabitants of Nightingale, it should be understood, have been convicted of serious crimes while under 17. On the generally accepted hypothesis that such young people should not be sent to penal custody, Nightingale would not exist. But with the law as it stands it is most impressive.

The young captain of their seven-a-side team had come to prison with a four-year sentence in an unusual way. His was not the old story of drugs and repeated petty crimes. He was living in a gypsy camp which was attacked by a gang of rival gypsies. A shoot-out followed. His 30-year-old brother killed someone; he himself, aged 15, inflicted a wound which led to his incarceration. What I discovered on this visit, however, was the strong Christian influence exerted in Nightingale by the officer in charge, a real evangelist. Recently, eight of his young people had gone up to London and had been baptized in a Baptist Church. I am not confident enough to say how much the admitted and indeed envied success of Nightingale is due to a Christian inspiration which the official world, even at its best, could hardly be expected to provide.

I next moved to the new wing for trouble-makers named after Lee Waite, where I was shown into a room with a tall, good-looking young man. 'I don't think we had better shut the door,' I said with mock nervousness. 'I might be bullied.' He quickly asserted that he had never bullied anyone in prison. (I learnt later from the prison psychologist that at least one bully admitted to 'intimidation', but not to bullying.) It happened, however, that this tall young man was a boxer who on his own admission had punched someone very hard in Lambeth Magistrates' Court. By an extraordinary chance, Governor Whitty saw this happening. The Governor told me that the man had terrified a young Pakistani. When he arrived in Feltham, the Governor then earmarked him for the new bullies' wing. As with others I spoke to that day, the young man insisted that drugs had been his downfall. He was in a remand wing and was expecting imprisonment, but he hoped and believed that he would be strong enough to resist drugs in future.

In this special wing, progress depends on obtaining marks for good conduct. An inmate may emerge after three weeks, but he may be there much longer if he does not conform. On the whole I was quite happy with the treatment of the young people, although in the first week they spend 23 hours out of 24 in their cells. No doubt it can be argued that the error of their ways must be forcibly brought home to them. But 23 hours out of 24 in a cell – is that Christianity? Or justice?

Finally, I visited the hospital, where I had a pleasant talk with another of these mild, soft-spoken youths in whose mouth you would not think butter would melt very quickly. He was facing a sentence of eight years for attempted rape. He insisted on his innocence, which I am in no position to assess. As in the earlier cases, he described drugs as his downfall. I had no doubt whatever that he needed a lot of help. He was being well looked after in the Feltham hospital, but when he moved to an adult prison what then?

I
Legal and Official Views

Dr Quentin Campbell

Metropolitan Stipendiary Magistrate

Apart from being a Metropolitan Stipendiary Magistrate, Dr Quentin Campbell acts as a Crown Court Recorder and speaks as a Chairman in the new Youth Courts. He is a law graduate of Oxford University and after qualifying as a solicitor served as a partner in a firm of solicitors in Oxford until 1980. While in practice, he explained, 98 per cent of his work was in respect of legal aid in criminal defence cases. In those days, he added, most Metropolitan Stipendiary Magistrates were barristers, whereas now there are more solicitors than barristers.

LORD LONGFORD: Do you follow different principles when sentencing young people under 21 years of age?

DR CAMPBELL: There are statutory provisions and there are different sentences available for those under 21.

LL: In practice, if two people – one of 19 and one of 23 – came before you, would you give the one under 19 less of a sentence?

QC: I might have to, even if I did not want to, because, as I say, there are restrictions on the way you deal with the under-21-year-olds. At under 21 they can't be sent to prison but must go to what is now called a young offender institution. One of the main differences is, of course, that a prison sentence can become a suspended sentence, but with the young offender institution you cannot grant suspension. From that point of view, one is often forced to give a custodial sentence, even if philosophically and humanely one did not want to sentence to custody.

These age limits are somewhat arbitrary, and if a 21-year-old and a 20-year-old have committed a nasty offence, morally there is no difference. But the younger a person is, the more one is looking towards the sort of sentence that will help to guide and instruct them, rather than anything else.

LL: I thought that you were very concerned for the future when I sat in your court. You showed a lot of concern for the welfare of the drug addicts.

QC: A lot of the people who appear are drug addicts, although they often deny it. Drug addicts go in for shop-lifting, and what they tend to steal is after-shave, smoked salmon, champagne and expensive men's suits, all of which happen to be items that obviously find a very quick sale in Soho. As soon as I see that somebody has been charged with stealing champagne and so on, and has previous convictions, I suspect that he is a drug addict.

LL: Would you consider that in general young offenders under 21 should be treated differently? That is official policy and it has been long established. I ought to tell you that I am well aware of the situation in Feltham. The Governor is a very sharp critic of the situation in these places.

QC: I share Joe Whitty's general views. The problem is, of course, that the way that young offenders are kept when they are in custody is quite dreadful. That is not to say necessarily that all young people can be allowed to roam about freely. There needs to be some sort of humane way, particularly bail. We get a lot of young gypsy children in London – 12–13 year-olds, boys and girls. They pickpocket and steal people's handbags; they hassle people, commit offence after offence while on bail. There is really nowhere to send them where there are restrictions on their liberty – for the very young ones, there is nowhere for them to go to. The older ones end up in somewhere like Feltham. But what do you do? There is a failure on the part of government to provide bail hostels.

LL: Yes indeed. I visited a bail hostel in Oxford recently. After 10.30 in the morning, they are completely free to roam about until 11.30 at night. I don't know whether that is true of all hostels. But, generally speaking, you agree with the idea that offenders under 21 should be treated differently from adults? This has been long established – since the introduction of the Borstal system.

QC: Because when one is dealing with young people they must be treated differently from adults; that is self-evident. I have had conversations over the years with Lucy Faithfull [Baroness Faithfull, see page 149] about this. She is very impressed with the Scottish

26

system. In Oxford, social services insist that one must work with the families, especially with 15–16 year-olds. The problem is that many of the youngest don't have families. It is statutory that the parent or guardian should come to court, but mostly if there is a family, nine times out of ten there is no father around and the mother goes out to work. She does not want to risk losing her job, or simply does not bother to appear in court.

LL: Joe Whitty says that Feltham is a troubled place – does that affect your sentencing policy?

QC: That is a point often raised in the juvenile court, as well as in the adult court – 'Don't send my client to prison, because these institutions are such dreadful places.'

LL: It is very much in my mind that bullying in young offender institutions is now so much worse than in adult prisons.

QC: But the truth is that you only send them to a young offender institution if you think the offence is so serious that you have a duty to impose the nastiest sanction the court has. These are very serious offences where one is only thinking in punitive terms – but they are very few. The only other time I would send a young person to prison is when they have a long history of offending and all other methods – probation, community service, IT [intermediate treatment] – have failed. They will then tend to end up inside. Although the magistracy really do look upon custody as the last possible thing to do, far too many Crown Court judges tend to think of custody as the first sentence rather than the last. I think of custody as very much the last resort. I consider as a sentencer that I am only sending young people into custody because of a serious offence and a history of offending in the past, and because they have not responded to every form of non-custodial sentence. If I reach that conclusion, the fact of prison conditions being awful seems to me totally irrelevant to my decision.

LL: Well, I have to take note of what you say.

QC: Would you not think that logical, if you put yourself in the position of the sentencer? You have formed the conclusion that the offence is so serious that a reasonable member of the public would expect the most heavy sentence available to the court, and really everything else has been tried and they took no notice?

LL: You were certainly showing so much concern when I was present—

QC: I am concerned as a sentencer. There are these small categories who will end up in custody. The places where they are held and the conditions under which they are held are matters of great concern, but do not affect my decision at all.

LL: Take one particular category – sex offenders. If a judge says, 'You will go to prison where you will receive proper treatment' – would they be getting some sort of treatment?

QC: Well, of course. That is not a particularly common offence by under-21-year-olds.

LL: I am mentioning in the House this afternoon the case of a young man of 26 who has just been given a life sentence for raping and strangling a young woman. When he was 15 he began to commit offences. He was put under supervision for a number of indecent assaults. Even with hindsight it is not easy to say what should have been done when he was 15. I am on the side of the Howard League and all such people who say that if he had been fairly treated he might have turned out better.

QC: I am on the side of the Howard League too, but if one gets a fellow like this, who is clearly in need of treatment and is a danger to the public, he must be sent somewhere where he will be treated and restricted. Where else can you send them?

LL: Indeed. So let us come along to youth matters. The people who come before you in the Juvenile Court – if they are not being sent to prison, where are they bring sent? I have been to a number of places – the Eton of these establishments is St Charles, where they have 90 staff to 30 inmates at a cost, they say, of £100,000 a year for each. Would you ever send anybody to St Charles at Brentwood?

QC: Wearing another hat, I am chairman of governors of Bessels Leigh, a special school near Oxford for up to 40 boys who are referred by local authorities and who have severe educational and other problems. All the boys get treatment, complete their schooling, get jobs and are totally transformed, with just the odd failure. All these special schools are intended to keep people away from courts. But this coming year we are going to be so down in numbers, for the first time in 30 years, that probably the whole future of the school will be in great jeopardy and it may well close. Local authorities cannot and will not refer the boys for financial reasons, so more young people will be coming into the court system and ending up in Feltham.

LL: Three boys of 15 recently raped a girl of 13 – would they come to your court?

28

QC: They would come to a Juvenile Court [now a Youth Court] which would have a discretion as to whether the case should be sent to the Crown Court. It is inevitable that a case of that nature would be sent to the Crown Court.

LL: This is a central point in the argument: where would they go?

QC: As I say, they would go to the Juvenile Court in the first place, and in the early stages at the Crown Court the question of bail would arise, because under the provisions of the 1991 Criminal Justice Act the idea is that boys of 17 and under should go to regional secure units provided by the local authorities. We are going to be up against the same problem with the local authorities: because of lack of funds, they won't have any regional secure units. And so your boys will end up back in Feltham.

LL: I am trying to go beyond the negative idea of keeping them out of prison. One view of the Home Office is that it is really better if you let the Probation Service deal with these young people.

QC: I have a tremendous respect for the Probation Service, but I have very limited respect for the social services departments of local authorities. The advantage of the Probation Service is that they have a history and training for court service. They are part of the court service, they understand the thinking of courts and put forward constructive and sensible proposals. The people in the social services cover such a wide field, they are not court-based. I would rather sympathize with the idea of using the Probation Service.

LL: It is an idea to be mulled over – that the future lies with the Probation Service.

QC: That is right. When the new Criminal Justice Act comes into force, it will require courts and sentencers and probation officers to work much more closely together than in the past. That is a very good thing, but I am afraid my brethren in the Crown Courts will find it difficult.

LL: I was very favourable to the White Paper *Punishment in the Community*. But the Probation Service do not like the word 'punishment'.

QC: They have rather changed their views. The new Criminal Justice Act coming into force in October [1992] does provide for punishment in the community, and although there was an initial reaction by the Probation Service, they have rather taken it on board now. There is within the social services departments, particularly with some of the London local authorities, a great resentment of courts.

29

The social services feel that courts represent awful Establishment figures. Therefore they put forward reports on young offenders which are often not helpful. They would perhaps say: 'This 16-year-old boy bumped an old lady on the head and left her lying on the pavement' and go on to suggest a conditional discharge. Whereas a Probation Service report will say: 'Undoubtedly the court will be thinking of custody, but we will put forward a constructive alternative.' The social services will suggest conditional discharge for quite serious offences, and because nothing is recommended, probably the boy will end up in detention. Then they will write a report and say: 'What an awful lot these courts are, sending these boys off to detention', and the blame will be put on the court.

LL: If you were a dictator and able to make vital changes, what would you wish to bring about?

QC: This is what we often talk about. It would probably require a lot of money being spent in providing some form of supervised care for those who, it was felt, could not be allowed to roam unsupervised in the community.

LL: That means many more probation officers.

QC: Probation hostels and secure children's homes, for want of a better word. To digress for a moment – the same applies to the vast number of mentally ill people I see in court.

LL: I think the Home Office want to do something about them.

QC: The mentally ill now appearing in court are often those who were in fairly awful long-stay Victorian mental hospitals and who were turned out to be cared for in the community. But in fact no care is given and they gravitate to the inner city where they turn up in my court, often charged with threatening behaviour. In reality they are thieving in the streets. This sort of person may well end up in custody on remand or sentence, and courts often get criticized in the Press. I don't sit there to send them to prison to be punished. They are not capable of looking after themselves; they need to be looked after. No hospital or social organization will touch them and they end up in prison. Quite deplorable.

   You asked me what I would do if I were a dictator. If I were, I would have lots of hostels for young offenders, with different degrees of security and supervision, and also lots of long-stay hostels for the mentally ill, which would be neither fully staffed hospitals in the proper sense nor prisons.

LL: Do you get many people with some kind of psychiatric trouble?

30

QC: Every Thursday we have a court psychiatrist in attendance, a very able man who runs a clinic in Soho. We were the first court in London to introduce this; it was our own initiative. During the course of the week anybody who is obviously mentally ill is held over until Thursday and he will see them, give a quick oral assessment. When somebody is seriously mentally ill and in need of inpatient treatment, he will eventually get them a bed somewhere.

LL: Since the closing of the mental hospitals the situation has been disastrous.

QC: Getting back to young offenders – I am a 90 per cent supporter of the Howard League and other penal reformers such as yourself. The 10 per cent where I would fall foul of you, I think, would be in a small number of cases where there is a need for symbolic punishment in the sentencing.

LL: I am a punishment man; but what have you in mind when you say 'symbolic punishment'?

QC: When a person commits a very nasty offence, right-thinking normal people would say: 'This is really nasty and therefore the court must impose the most severe sentence, which is always custody.' Whether or not he comes out worse than when he went in seems to me irrelevant. In most such cases one imposes the most severe sentence, the most severe punishment, because the public expect it.

LL: We are all familiar with the deterrent argument – that people must be punished when they rob a bank—

QC: The deterrent element so far as robbing a bank is concerned does not really exist. The person who commits a serious offence is not remotely deterred. The element of deterrence in a sentence is almost nil. The fear of going to prison may deter someone from stealing in Woolworth's, but in reality they would not be sent to prison. The serious criminal is never deterred.

LL: I must question you upon this need to pay attention to the public. You are probably aware of my attitude to the release of Myra Hindley. Are you saying that she should not be released because of possible public outcry?

QC: I would be entirely with you so far as that particular issue is concerned. I do not think that what people are saying is that the public would not stomach her release. What they are really saying is that some people would protest most volubly. They are the sort of people who take extreme views on the abolition of hanging and all

31

the rest of it. One does not pander to them. But again, take the case of a young man with a string of convictions who hangs around a post office, sees an old lady get her pension, then bashes her on the head, steals her money and runs off. If the public read that he got a conditional discharge or something unduly lenient, then the public reasonably think that is wrong – and I think so too. Forgetting Myra Hindley, you must have experienced, as I have, that prisoners themselves have very hard views on crime and punishment. I often used to say to my clients: 'What would you do, Jim, if you were a judge in your case?' He would reply: 'I would give me five years!'

LL: Judges, I like to think, stand for justice – and do not give way to mob rule.

QC: But how does one define justice? Justice is doing what is seen by most people – most reasonable people – as a fair way of applying the rules of society. As a matter of interest, how would you define justice?

LL: I would say that it is what God would do in their place. I know that in practice the judge cannot behave like that. But the symbolic element sticks in my throat.

QC: May I just stress that symbolic punishment would only apply in a very small number of cases, cases of very extreme nastiness.

LL: How far would feeling aroused against a defendant in the press influence you in your sentencing?

QC: I would never, I hope, take a view that I must find a way of not sending this person to prison, because the public are going to create an uproar. But if I were dealing with a child-molester, the public may well be baying for blood, and I would be sitting there with the benefit of medical and psychiatric reports, would read about the defendant's appalling background, his own history of child abuse, sexual abuse and so on, and that there was a constructive alternative by way of treatment. People would say that he ought to be locked up and the key thrown away, but I would not do it. I would try to put him on probation, with a view to psychiatric treatment. Every sentencer has to be arrogant to the extent that he must do what is fair and not fall in with public outcry.

LL: I suppose you have to consider the credibility of the judicial system?

QC: You are trying to do what is just and fair. Sometimes it does coincide with public outcry. At the end of the day, if you disagreed with anything I did, you would at least understand why I did it.

LL: I think tremendous care is taken. The other day I went to a Juvenile Court. There was a man found guilty many times of stealing. The judge and chairman withdrew and the two social workers said, 'It seems like custody.' But he was given another chance. I do realize that people are very reluctant to send young offenders to custody.

Is there anything you would like to say in general about the treatment of young offenders today?

QC: The only major area where you and I probably part company concerns the needs of the young offender. His or her problems are a very major element in sentencing, but not necessarily the be-all and end-all of sentencing.

Robin Pearse Wheatley

Crown Court Recorder

Robin Pearse Wheatley is a barrister of long experience, a Recorder of the Crown Court and a former school governor. He is married, with three young children.

LORD LONGFORD: You have had a lot of practical experience of young offenders. Do you feel that, as a Recorder, you draw a distinction between the way in which you sentence young offenders and adult ones? Do you think a line should be drawn between them?

ROBIN PEARSE WHEATLEY: I certainly feel that there is a very great distinction between adult and young offenders. My personal concern is that, inevitably, if there is legislation to distinguish between young and adult offenders, an arbitrary line must be drawn at a particular age. This is something which has troubled me greatly. For example, I have had a number of clients over the years who have been desperate to get into court quickly, because their twenty-first birthday was coming up. It is an absurd situation – that a man can expect his sentence to be substantially reduced by virtue of the fact that he comes up in court shortly before his twenty-first birthday.

LL: Nevertheless, you think that some line has to be drawn?

RPW: It is inevitable. I think, however, that the government has recognized the problem in the 1991 Criminal Justice Act, particularly where the court can consider passing what is known as a community sentence. A community sentence is a probation order, supervision order or a community sentence order.

LL: Not a fine or anything else?

34

RPW: No, nothing else. The court, incidentally, will be assisted as to the maturity of the person to be sentenced, and I think this is a most important factor indeed.

LL: That is interesting.

RPW: In the new Act there are a number of aspects which are particularly interesting.

LL: You are very encouraged by this new Act in that respect?

RPW: In that respect, yes. For example: 17-year-olds, who previously would have been considered as young adults, are now to be dealt with by what is called the Youth Court. The courts will be assisted, and virtually no sentence will be passed in future without their being a report—

LL: No custodial sentence?

RPW: No custodial sentence. Under the provision of the Act, and I quote:

When a court decides to pass a community sentence on an offender of any age it must ensure that the sentence matches the seriousness of the offence, and that the particular sentence imposed is the one which is the most suitable for the offender. In deciding which is the most suitable community sentence for a 16 or 17 year-old, courts will need to take account of the offender's circumstances and of the stage of his/her emotional, intellectual, social and physical development in the transition from childhood to adulthood. This decision will be a particularly difficult one to make. Factors which are likely to be relevant include:

the offender's continuing dependence on or independence from his or her parents;

whether he/she is leading a stable independent life, and has family responsibilities of his/her own;

whether he/she is still in full-time education or in or seeking employment;

the general pattern of his/her social behaviour and his/her leisure interests and activities;

the nature of his/her relationship with friends and associates;

whether he/she accepts personal responsibility for his/her actions;

his/her attitude towards the offence and any victims;

whether he/she is intellectually impaired.

Information about and assessment of these factors in pre-sentence reports will be particularly helpful to the courts in reaching their decision.

One of my particular concerns with reference to the foregoing is that all of these factors should be taken into consideration by *all* courts when dealing with young offenders under 18 years of age, as a matter of course. They should not be limited to 16–17 year-olds.

In these matters, the Act focuses on a fundamental difficulty for juvenile and indeed adult courts when dealing with the young offender. It has been my experience that you can have a 21-year-old who is hopelessly immature, and there is no real logic in treating him or her differently from an 18-year-old.

LL: Who is going to be the judge of this maturity or immaturity?

RPW: It was my practice in the years when I was an Assistant Recorder that if I had a report from a probation office who was dealing with a young person, I nearly always, if possible, had the probation officer in court and asked him: 'Have you been able to form an assessment of the maturity of the person we are dealing with?' I found that very helpful.

LL: I agree that this question of maturity is an important issue.

RPW: It is part and parcel of a much wider problem. Young people who have had a disrupted background, or an inadequate one, simply do not understand the rules of social behaviour in the way that most people do. If you go to Feltham, they will tell you that their task is almost irrelevant to the offence which brought the young person there. They see their role as teaching them the fundamentals of social behaviour. The structure of Feltham, with its punishments and rewards, is intended to instil social behaviour into youngsters who simply do not understand that what they are doing is unacceptable, and is likely to affect other people adversely. I feel that all prison officers, especially those dealing with young people, should have a sense of vocation and be much more highly trained than they tend to be at present. We cannot give up on our young people.

LL: Would you say that there should be some special responsibility for parents and guardians? If so, in the case of what young people?

RPW: The new Criminal Justice Act requires parents and guardians to attend court with their children, if the children are under 18 years of age – in other words, everybody who comes before the Youth Court. I think this is absolutely essential because, too often, in punishing the young person it is a matter really of attacking the symptom and not the cause – and the cause more often than not is the parents themselves. If you don't bring them into the process, it is hopeless to try to bring home to the offender that what he or she is doing is wrong.

LL: Putting it crudely, you hope parents will be led to behave better?

RPW: It is essential for our society that parents should be as fully aware of their responsibilities in respect of their children as they possibly can be. If they can just wash their hands of their children, knowing full well that those children, often at a quite young age, are out on the streets at night, the devil finding work for idle hands, then that surely must be irresponsible to the point almost of being criminal.

LL: This is in the Act, is it?

RPW: I go much further than the Act. There is no suggestion there of criminalizing parental behaviour.

LL: How would you go further than the Act?

RPW: Let me just comment on it. I am entirely in favour of it. Very often you find that children who commit offences simply do not know their father; the mother sometimes does not know who the father is. They come from one-parent families. The number of young offenders with a normal, stable family background is probably very small. But even so, whatever the problems, even if the mother is an object of pity, having made a terrible mess of her life, she must be involved in the process. It is hopeless to have a parent who is one step away from the court proceedings.

LL: What age are we speaking of?

RPW: I am speaking about the Youth Court – up to 18 years of age. I think all of this in the new Act is to be welcomed. How it will work in practice is another thing. You and I would find it very odd that a parent would not want to come to court when a child is in trouble.

LL: I have known plenty of 16–17 year-olds, through my long association with the New Horizon Centre, who were living away from home. I don't know what you do about them – a good many of these young people are homeless. What do you do about adolescents who have left home?

RPW: I think the courts should have the power – and they probably do have – to order the offender to return home pending trial.

LL: But many of these young people have come from Glasgow, for example—

RPW: It is very often the fact that they left home which led to their getting into trouble in the first place. On the other hand, there are

37

often great tensions at home. Many leave home because they are being abused. It is a great problem.

LL: Yes, indeed.

RPW: But somebody must take responsibility for all young offenders, in my view. The court should ask the question: Who is the most appropriate person to take responsibility for this young person pending trial? The court should hear representations – including very often the wishes of the young person as well – as to where they should go. In many cases that will be to the care of the local authority, if it is not practical for the parents to take responsibility. We think that there should be appointed for every young offender a person who has, if not a responsibility, then availability. It may very well be a probation officer or local authority official. Where there is no realistic prospect of a parent taking responsibility for a young person pending trial, there should always be somebody to oversee and guide them. It is unacceptable for a young offender, who may have committed some quite minor offence, simply to be released on bail. I know that they will have legal advice, but there is no guarantee that somebody will look after them. They may go home and not tell their parents. They may well tell their parents a completely false account of what has happened. Parents might be appalled if they knew the full truth.

LL: That is quite a big idea—

RPW: You have got to have somebody responsible for that young person until the day of the disposal of their case.

LL: What about afterwards – after they have been sentenced?

RPW: The court will make a community order or whatever. The court automatically considers what has to be done.

LL: So the remand period is the crucial one?

RPW: It is in the remand period that so many further offences get committed.

LL: Let us pursue the question of the responsible person for a moment. On the one hand, I suppose, this person is appointed with the approval of the offender and with their own consent?

RPW: The accused person can make representations. For example, he may say: 'Please don't send me back home; my father beats me.' And the court should taken notice of that. If the court finds – and it may have a wide discretion in this – that the child has oppressive parents, it should not send him back. It should be quite possible to draw up guidelines whereby the court would not send a child back where there is a suggestion of abusive behaviour.

LL: Should the responsible person be a volunteer? If some State official is appointed, he has to do it.

RPW: One of the anomalies in Youth Court proceedings is that, whereas the Youth Court will deal with alleged offenders up to the age of 18, bail provisions for 17-year-olds come under the old provisions for young offenders, rather than children. I cannot see any difficulty about this. The period between arrest and disposal of the case is a crucial period. Time and time again these young people commit further offences in the interim, and who is responsible? If the police catch them they will be arrested again, but the chances are that they will not be caught.

LL: Take somebody sent off to Feltham on remand – would there be somebody responsible for him as distinct from a member of staff?

RPW: In some cases, the young offender will be kept in custody and there will be somebody responsible for him. It may be that a person in custody should have a particular probation officer assigned to him or her at an early stage. There is a strong argument for that. The thing that really bothers me, and ought to bother everybody, is that if these young people are released without any control into the community, and if there is no realistic prospect of the parents exercising any control, then it is highly likely that they will continue to offend.

LL: You are talking of people on bail?

RPW: On bail. No young offender should be released and left to his own devices. Somebody should monitor his progress during this period. It should not be an oppressive matter. I foresee such a person as a probation officer.

LL: The young offender would have to report regularly, wouldn't he, to say the least?

RPW: Even if he is sent to a bail hostel, there should be a named person who is responsible for him.

LL: You mean a member of the staff of the bail hostel?

RPW: Anybody who is appropriate. But where the offence is minor, it may be that the court will say: This is a minor offence and it is not necessary for a responsible person to be appointed. If, however, the offender has a history of offending, he is absconding from school, or there is reason to believe that he is immature and out of control, there should be somebody to keep an eye on him while on bail. There must be many instances where the court does not think that the gravity of the offence is serious enough to justify supervision, despite the type of person involved. Nevertheless, in this important period when people are awaiting trial, they should not be released into the community without being monitored.

LL: Just to clarify your argument: you are not saying that when the young person is brought to court, just before being sentenced, a parent or such-like should be produced?

RPW: Oh yes, I am. That is the law: Sections 56–58 of the new Act state that the parent must be present when the child is under 18. What I am saying is that in those rare cases where there is a responsible parent, they should be present. It should always be made clear to those parents – and this goes beyond the Act – that they have a responsibility, so far as they are able, to ensure the well-being and good behaviour of their children.

There are cases where it is not realistic for the parent to come to court – they may live miles away, or the family may be a wholly inadequate single-parent one where the mother goes out to work, that sort of thing. The law says that the child should be with a friend, and the friend is often an officer of the local authority or Probation Service. This should be extended further: if the Probation Service or the local authority is providing someone to go to court with the young offender, it should not simply be a matter of turning up at the court on the day, there should be a monitoring process.

LL: If the Prime Minister or Home Secretary asked you to bring about reforms, is there anything you would want to see done?

RPW: I would trust judges and magistrates a little more than is the practice these days. Criticisms are nearly always ill-informed; the critic can never be as fully informed as the judge or magistrate who is trying the case and who has access to information which the press cannot have. Very often, the criticisms of the judge are an outcome of the regulation of his powers brought about as a result of earlier criticisms. There have been some very strong criticisms of judges lately – for sending young people to short periods of imprisonment for reckless driving, for instance. Now the difficulty the judges face, which the public seldom hear about, is that the sentencing power of the judge is limited. At the moment death by reckless driving attracts a sentence of five years, and unless the offence is the worst possible type of its kind, the sentence must be less than five years. Again, if the defendant pleads guilty, considerably less than five years.

As a result of increased legislation, sentencing, which is always regarded as an art rather than a science by those who do it, is getting more and more complicated. Inevitably there will come a point where legislation becomes counter-productive, and we have probably reached that point now. I would not like to see any further regulation which effectively boxes in magistrates and judges, when we should be relying on their goodwill and experience to pass the best possible sentence in every case.

What worries me particularly is that the most elaborate system for dealing with young offenders comes to nought if they simply do not care what happens to them. This is what I call the politics of despair. Such young people simply do not care what the judges say, because they have no respect for authority. They do not care if they are put into custody, because they have a pretty miserable home life anyway. It does not bother them if they are placed on community service, because it is only another way of passing the time, and if they don't like it, they won't do it. There is simply nothing the courts can do with them.

No society, however, can turn its back on such people because they are *young* people.

Judge Stephen Tumim
Her Majesty's Chief Inspector of Prisons

Judge Stephen Tumim has been HM Chief Inspector of Prisons since 1987. He was called to the Bar in 1955 and went on to be a Recorder of the Crown Court and a Judge of Willesden County Court. He is a man of audacious, even iconoclastic, spirit, and he is a man of culture, among many other interests having been Chairman of the Friends of the Tate from 1983 to 1990.

LORD LONGFORD: Should young offenders, between the ages of 17 and 20 years or younger, be treated in some way differently from adults?

STEPHEN TUMIM: I have no doubt that they should be treated differently. I don't think they are treated sufficiently differently. The training aspect of imprisonment, which I put the highest importance on, applies even more when dealing with that group than with any other group.

What do I think about training, what do I want prisons to do? I am not dealing at the moment with the maniacal side of it, with the mass murderer or terrorist, just with the ordinary common or garden criminal, usually a young man between the ages of 18 and 30 who is a burglar or similar offender. They have two troubles: first, they have failed at school, or school has failed them. They don't know anything. Second, they have not made normal family relationships, or relationships with the other sex which are sensible and which work.

This group makes up the majority of prisoners. What I want to do with them is to give them training. I see prisons as having the obvious functions of security, otherwise they are not prisons. But

42

the clear function of the Prison Service is to show care and humanity towards prisoners. Then there is training. Training has three sections. One is, so to speak, academic training, which is training in a skill to earn money and is very often remedial education, reading and writing. Second, social skills. They begin with relationships, drink, drugs, AIDS, all that, as well as how to conduct day-to-day life – budgeting, job interviews and so on. The third aspect, important with the young and all prisoners to a different degree, is that they should have continuing support when they go back into the community. Continuing support is not just going to come from care workers such as probation officers. It is going to come, and it has got to come, from links with family and community.

LL: But what about those who have the most awful family – or none at all?

ST: When Lord Justice Woolf spoke in his report about community prisons, what he meant was not some elaborate new bricks and mortar, but to get as many prisoners as possible, particularly young offenders, within reach of the family community from which they came. Unless you have those links strengthened – it is not just a question of bringing them together, but actually strengthening them – then an offender's chance of getting support in the community to put his new training into effect is very much diminished. In essence, I look at family links not so much under the heading of care and humanity, but under the heading of training. All these matters apply more highly to young offenders than to anybody else in the system.

The immediate concern I have with young offenders is that I would like to see a very big campaign for the fuller training of staff dealing with them. It is common sense that untrained officers who have spent much of their time with older, hardened criminals will have great difficulty at first with adolescents. You are also calling on prison governors, who may have spent many years of their careers in high-security prisons. You are now putting them in charge of the care and training of adolescents, much as a headmaster would be, but without any preparation. I am asking for *real training* in dealing with youth.

I am using the word 'training' in its widest possible sense. I want training in security and care; I want much more straight training for staff and governors. I don't think a few weeks here and there on a course is adequate. We need youth workers, the sort used to running youth clubs, people like that.

LL: Youth workers – are you suggesting that they would join the Prison Service?

43

ST: No. I think they could be brought in to train staff.

LL: And you think governors should be trained too?

ST: Governors certainly should. I want much more focus on young offender institutions as a particular form of schooling to stop people going back time and time again. I repeat that I am talking here of the ordinary decent criminal – what is known in Northern Ireland as the ODC.

LL: Take the case in today's *Times*: two young men found guilty of a particularly vicious assault on an old lady. One got ten years in prison, while the other nine years in a young offender institution. Would you say one is presumably over 21 and the other younger?

ST: Yes. It was in fact a boy of 17.

LL: Well, obviously nothing is perfect, but would you say that if you are over 21 you get a different kind of treatment?

ST: The older young man, who is presumably over 21, probably got a year longer because he was older and more experienced. But these two don't come within my ODC set-up.

LL: Are you in sympathy with the language the judge used? He called them 'nasty, cowardly, undersized little bodies'.

ST: One can be critical over it, but what he was doing is one of the functions of a senior judge, which is to make a statement of denunciation in support of the law. Although it may be unattractive, I think it has got to be done from time to time. I am in sympathy with him on this sentence.

LL: Coming back to the issue: would you agree that young offenders like those two should be treated differently from adults?

ST: Yes, but it is a question of degree. Take somebody who, the most careful assessment says, simply can't be trained – you have to move towards humane restraint to some extent.

LL: Even with young fellows? You can't give up hope, surely?

ST: I am not going to give up hope very readily, but you have to look at the skills of the teachers and see what you can do. These boys seem to me appallingly difficult.

LL: Have you inspected Feltham lately? They claim that the staff is totally inadequate by 40 places.

ST: I said in my report on Feltham that I appreciated that they claim to be short by this very large number of people. What I want is a proper professional assessment by an area manager of what their precise requirements are. With shortage of staff it can be a failure of disposition of staff, or genuine shortage, or again it can be a bit of a try-on to get more staff for the sake of getting more staff. I am not in a position to assess; that is the job of my management. If the Governor says that he really is short by a huge number, then the Home Office should set up a team of professionals to assess precisely what his needs are.

LL: Why?

ST: Why? Because other governors get senior and experienced Prison Service assessors who say 'Do you need a man standing there?' or 'Do you need two people on education?' This is a technical exercise.

LL: Joe Whitty [the Governor of Feltham] was criticized for failing to produce a number of people in court. When I asked him about it, he said: 'I have not got the staff to send people to court. We would have to keep everyone locked up even longer.' That is the situation.

ST: There is an element of truth in that, which is one of the reasons why the Woolf Report favoured Criminal Justice Committees where at least we bring together judges and prison governors to explain their problems to each other. It is the lack of communication between these branches of criminal justice which is one of the fundamental things wrong. A criminal justice system means a system in which everybody knows what the others are saying. The basic difficulty is that we don't have one in England because judges, prison governors, senior prosecutors and the Probation Service don't meet and discuss their problems with each other. Woolf favoured very strongly that they should.

Since the Woolf Report was presented, the Home Office has accepted this and has set up a national committee. The new Lord Chief Justice has agreed to local committees, with the local circuit judge and the governor of the local prison—

LL: Yes, but to get back to Feltham. How do you decide whether they are allocating staff efficiently?

ST: If you are writing about young offenders, you want to look much more broadly than at Feltham which is an extreme case in many ways. My report on Aylesbury came out yesterday. I went there last summer and delivered my report very quickly. Aylesbury is a young offender institution for long-term offenders. In other words, the two young men we have just been speaking of would go there rather than to Feltham. It is for convicted young offenders

45

who are dangerous or who would be potentially a danger if they did escape. The toughest of young offenders tend to go to Aylesbury nationally.

It follows that we have the same problem there as we have with Dartmoor and, to some extent, with Feltham. You are taking people right away from their community and their family. More and more I tend to worry about doing that. I see the difficulty of confining long-term prisoners, and visits are very difficult. What is interesting about Aylesbury is that it works frightfully well in education, largely because there is a very alert governor, a former teacher. There are certain weaknesses. There is a lack of work in the workshops, the kitchens are not too good, visits are not too good either, and various other things are wrong. But essentially he is concentrating on education, saying that this is a place for young offenders and consequently that teaching them is a first priority.

Aylesbury has got many things against it – problems of size, space, security, muddle over control of young offenders – but going for it is a committed staff and governor who work well with the prisoners and have a good relationship with them. Education is given top priority. With young offenders, I would look always for the educational side of training to be given a very high priority.

LL: Yes, but two-thirds of those in Feltham are on remand. Remand prisoners cannot be made to do anything – those that I saw were just lying in their beds.

ST: This is a question of leadership. You can't make people learn, can you? But there has to be a voluntary element in education. I think we make a great mistake – most countries make a great mistake – about remand prisoners. If you are going to leave people on remand for about a year sometimes, particularly very young people, they must be offered schooling, kept occupied. Saying 'You can't make them do it' just leads on to 'Therefore we don't offer it'. Very misguided. What these people need is leadership, more old-fashioned leadership. I have come across prisons where everybody is active and does things. Where you find that, you find an active governor.

LL: I would like to ask a general question about Borstal. The Borstal system was abolished. It was based on training. Has training disappeared with it? Wasn't it a great pity that the Borstal system and its philosophy were abolished?

ST: I think so. But I also think it is a great pity that English society has changed in certain respects. You cannot revive Borstal as it was in the culture of the 1990s. I don't think it fits in. Ruggles-Brise

46

started it in early Edwardian days, giving the sort of leadership that later officers' cadet corps gave. I think my idea of training – as I was saying earlier, the three types – can be made effective today, but I think the leadership system of Borstal is unacceptable to our present culture. It is as simple as that.

LL: There is a strong demand by many people, including the Howard League and NACRO, that 15-year-olds should be kept out of custody. Some go further and say that 16–18 year-olds should be sent to special units, not to penal custody. Then the question arises: Where do you send them?

ST: I am interested in this problem and I am very concerned about it. First, age is very difficult. You get mature 16-year-olds and immature 17 and 18-year-olds.

LL: People say they can go to local secure units, but I think the Probation Service would be better qualified to deal with them, even if it meant having some kind of probation hostels. For dealing with young delinquents, probation officers are better trained than the local authority people.

ST: Yes, I think this is right. What worries me about it is that, if you take the middle teens – 15–16 year-olds – and you put them in a local authority institution, they very easily go into a grey, murky Edwardian house buried somewhere in the suburbs and nobody keeps an eye on them. I am not defending the young offender institutions, but at least they are regularly inspected and somebody keeps an eye on them. I am a little worried about local authority institutions. In a secluded home in a leafy suburb, goodness knows what happens behind the curtains, and there is no proper inspection.

LL: So you would agree that 15-year-olds should be kept out of custody? And would you say that 16–17 year-olds should also be kept out of prison custody?

ST: As penal custody is at present, yes. If, in fact, you change the nature of these places and turn them into really good, caring, training places, which fill the gaps in the upbringing of the young offenders which school and family have failed to fill, then I feel the position must change.

Winifred Tumim

Chairman of the Youth Treatment Service Committee

Winifred Tumim is married to Judge Stephen Tumim. In addition to her chairmanship of the Secretary of State for Health's Youth Treatment Service Committee, she is Chairman of the Royal National Institute for the Deaf, Chairman of the Trustees of the Independent Living Fund (a government-funded charity which enables disabled people to live in the community instead of in residential homes), and a Magistrate on the Family Panel.

LORD LONGFORD: Let's begin with youth treatment centres. I have been to one, St Charles in Brentwood. I understand that there is another, Glenthorne near Birmingham. Are there more than two? Is your Youth Treatment Service Committee just looking into these?

WINIFRED TUMIM: Only two so far. St Charles was set up first and then Glenthorne. Our remit is to oversee the homes with particular reference to the rights of the young people in them. Ours is a standing committee – permanent – and one of our jobs is to establish what the rules are and to see that they are kept. We spend our time looking at the records, tracking complaints from beginning to end and making sure that they are dealt with expeditiously.

Although there are only 30 boys at St Charles, for instance, the staff-to-pupil rate is large and, as you probably know, the cost per person per year is vast. The set-up is complex and there is a great deal of work. We talk to the young people, find out how they feel about their treatment and make sure that the education is appropriate.

Now, with Stephen, I visit two St Charles graduates who went on to Aylesbury Prison – that is a fascinating point. Some of the young

48

people go on from a treatment centre to a prison – an absurd situation.

LL: You mean that they go to prison to finish their sentence?

WT: It may be indeterminate. Some, for instance, are sentenced at 16 and if the Parole Board do not see fit, they go on from St Charles or Glenthorne to a young offender institution or prison. As I said, this is an absurd situation. It is odd to sentence somebody at 14, say, for a one-off murder and at 18 or 19 he ends up in Aylesbury, when the treatment is harsher than it was directly after the crime was committed. That is somehow paradoxical.

LL: When I was at Feltham recently, news came through that three boys had been convicted of raping a girl of 13. I don't know whether it is fair to ask you what should be done about them. They might, I suppose, have found themselves at St Charles?

WT: This is a worrying area. What happens is that if they are 15 or 16, they will be allocated either to a young offender institution or a local authority secure unit. The decision is made by the Home Office on the basis of an assessment by the Department of Health. They will make a recommendation that X is a suitable candidate meeting some of the criteria – and they are tough criteria – for going to one of the youth treatment centres or secure units rather than a penal institution.

LL: Do you think that, on the whole, the decision is made in the best way possible?

WT: It is at the moment, given that the number of places in secure units is a very small proportion. On the other hand, if there were more places in secure institutions, more young people would benefit from them.

LL: On the face of it, St Charles is the ideal places for treatment. Going round it – it's a lovely place.

WT: No doubt it is. But the thing about the centres which is interesting is that the Dartington Social Research Unit of Bristol University does a considerable amount of research into the outcome – in other words, they evaluate the treatment to ascertain how successful it is. They also go to young offender institutions to see them in practice. There is a small group of young offenders at these institutions – about the same number as at St Charles and Glenthorne – who, if there were enough facilities, would have been eligible to go to a treatment centre. In other words, if all those who meet the criteria were to go to youth treatment centres, there should be double the number of places available.

LL: At £100,000 each a year, you mean?

WT: There is only a small number of people – 180 perhaps. In a humane and compassionate society, young people who have committed serious crimes as a result, in the main, of having been damaged themselves, deserve the best possible treatment.

LL: You think the present arrangements in this respect are satisfactory, if sufficient places were available?

WT: If you apply the tough set of criteria, the number of young people meeting them would call for double the number of places now available to provide the treatment – and treatment is the key word. What I have not mentioned is that there will be a number who are too young to go to young offender institutions – say, the 12-year-old muggers – but they are very few and far between.

LL: Are the staff qualified at St Charles?

WT: In the Youth Treatment Service, the group workers are all fully qualified, but the social workers not necessarily so. The staff come from a variety of disciplines – they may be psychiatric nurses, teachers, social workers and so on. There are quite a number of psychologists and psychiatrists, too. They are well paid, much better so than in other institutions, and being well resourced the Service attracts a good calibre of staff.

Going back to the question of research results. What encourages me to believe in them is that the prognosis in respect of those who have committed serious one-off crimes is better than it would have been if they had been sent to a young offender institution.

LL: How do you go about your investigations at these places?

WT: There are five of us in the group. We are to some extent opportunists. We focus on, say, education, drop in on classes, see the inspectors, read the reports, talk to the young people, have a meal, talk to the cooks. We inspect the returns, look into the single separations – how often they are used, ask why, talk to those concerned, ask how they feel about it. We then go back and report.

LL: Forgive my saying so, but it is rather a sad state of affairs if your committee is looking after only two institutions. If you told me you were looking after half a dozen—

WT: We have already sussed out quite a lot. We have a good group.

50

LL: Looking at it more broadly, are these treatment centres the right answer for a large number of young offenders? Is the Department of Health a better bet than local authorities? How do you see the future, if you had your way – if you were a dictator?

WT: Double the number of young people should be given this sort of Rolls-Royce treatment, without it being a waste of money. Much as I would like to do the same thing for every young person in a young offender institution, it plainly cannot be done.

LL: We are talking of the under-17s, or the under-18s under the new Criminal Justice Act?

WT: Yes. The local authority secure institutions that do exist will be taking some of the characters we might have had. In the main, we have the most difficult ones in the Youth Treatment Service, so Aycliffe, Eastmore and the other long-term secure institutions will not be catering for such seriously difficult young people.

LL: Do you think local authorities are capable of providing these places? In the secure units of children's homes that I have visited, there are unqualified people in charge.

WT: On the whole, local authorities are not the right people, partly because no single local authority will have enough young people to justify it. You need consortia. I don't think they can resource it properly. It has to be funded centrally and also needs to be managed on an agency basis.

LL: An agency?

WT: The chief executive or whoever is in charge should have much more control over his budgets and his own management. The funds should come from the Department of Health and not the local authority, who would not take the service on anyway – why should they? They have neither the money nor the expertise. It must be done properly.

LL: Now I am going to raise a wider question, which I only touched on earlier – the role of the Probation Service. I have the impression that quite a lot of people in the Home Office believe that the future of looking after young delinquents lies more with the Probation Service who, after all, are trained to deal with delinquency. In the end we are left with the question: Who is going to look after these young people?

WT: When they leave?

LL: While they are there. The Probation Service are trained to deal with delinquency; local authority people are not.

WT: Not in relation to this group – probation people have not got the training.

LL: The Probation Service have the same training as social workers – they have the same qualifications.

WT: If a probation officer wanted to stop being a probation officer and came to work at St Charles, I think he would be excellent. I would have no quarrel with that. But I don't think it is the role of the Probation Service. They are not necessarily expert with young people. The reason it comes under the Department of Health is that it is to do with children, and you need to know about child development.

LL: The 16–17 year-olds who have committed murder and so on – we know they should not go to prison. I don't think the staff of a local authority are trained for this sort of thing. The Probation Service are trained.

WT: With the generality of young criminals – the average person who comes before me on the Bench – I would totally agree with you. But the sort of people in the Youth Treatment Service are quite positively different from the average.

LL: Well, you had 90 staff when I last went to St Charles. What are they? Are they social workers?

WT: No, they are a mixture of psychiatric nurses, qualified social workers, teachers for maladjusted children. The group workers come from a variety of backgrounds.

LL: To put it in the simplest way: Who is to take responsibility for these young people – the Department of Health or the local authority?

WT: I have no enthusiasm for local authorities. They do not have the resources, they do not have the incentive. None of them has enough people to develop something which would be really good. Probably we ought to try a mixture of different models and see what works. I would like to see more collaboration between the Department of Health and the Home Office – that is a very important area.

LL: There should be much more co-ordination between the Department of Health and the Home Office.

WT: There is no simple answer. You could have experiments with jointly funded projects, which might be run by the Probation Service in one area, or might be run by an enlightened consortium of local authorities, properly supervised by the Department of Health. I would explore different models – have two or three different kinds to see which was the most beneficial. As nothing could be more disastrous than what we have got, a few judicious and cautious experiments might well find the right answer.

LL: This will become more relevant with the new Youth Court – you will have people up to 18 coming in, and the numbers will be much greater. And yet where do you send them? I think if left to local authorities, it won't be done. We have got to create some new institutions.

WT: Yes. There is the Children Act and the Criminal Justice Act – these two new Acts should be a great help—

LL: The responsibility should fall on the Department of Health?

WT: I think so, much more. They have the expertise in child development; they know about young people. The Home Office have a different perspective, a more punitive outlook. The Home Office will always have an interest.

Mary Tuck

Former Director of the Home Office Research and Planning Unit

In my book *Punishment and the Punished* I introduced Mary Tuck as a married lady with four children, highly qualified academically as a criminologist, with a Master's degree in Social Psychology, among others, and as a former Director of the Home Office Research and Planning Unit. She has since became a member of the Parole Board, as well as of the Council of the ESRC (Economic and Social Research Council), a social-science research body handing out government grants. She is also engaged in a research initiative on domestic violence, with a view to bringing about a common policy between women's aid and child abuse groups. Her services in research have brought her a CBE.

Mary Tuck explained that two reasons for the increase in crime figures in recent years are, first, that domestic violence, child abuse and even rape were formerly outside the scope of the criminal justice system; and second that domestic violence is now much more widely reported. Wives are no longer expected to put up with brutal treatment.

LORD LONGFORD: Should young offenders, however you define them, be treated differently from adults?

MARY TUCK: Very much. One of the most important things in the Criminal Justice Act of 1991 is the setting up of Youth Courts and grouping 18-year-olds with the 17-year-olds. I think undoubtedly this switch in the age at which they now come to the Juvenile Courts will help, because the Juvenile Court makes less use of custody than the ordinary courts. Other countries cut their prison population

54

figures down by not naming them as juveniles and putting them in prison less.

LL: Take the recent case of a young man of 26 with a history of violent crime and sexual assault since he was 16 who, after being released on bail on another rape charge, raped and murdered a young woman. He has now been jailed for life. Do you agree that it was right just to put him under supervision, or should he have been put into some sort of custody?

MT: It is knocking on an open door to say: 'Don't put them in prison under 16' – that is accepted. They are to go into regional secure units run by the local authority. Your point that it has to be custody is right. But NACRO would say that it is whether you think of the children as being in child care or being in prison. Feltham has a ratio of 2 inmates to 1 staff, but the child-care ration is 4 staff to 1 inmate. So it makes a difference. Compare these figures with those of a public school – 9 boys to 1 staff. Prison staffing ratios have gone up the whole of this century. The difference between prison and child custody is the difference in the nature of the staff – the training of the staff and the number of staff per inmate.

The answer is care in the community and intensive probation. You raised the question of the young man jailed for life. This is the problem. How do you deal with the young criminal? I strongly believe that trying to train the young offender is useless. What he has got to learn is how to live, day by day, in the community. These boys are the deprived of the deprived. They don't know how to live. There are some extremely good schemes being developed in intensive probation – a new development to probation work.

LL: Are you talking of residential places?

MT: I have here an interim report on this subject in which it is explained that 'intensive probation programmes [should be set up] exclusively for offenders who would otherwise receive custodial sentences. The courts should be involved closely in the design of the programme and the police should be kept in touch. The projects should be monitored, costed and evaluated.' The basic idea arose out of the White Papers of five to six years ago on punishment in the community. There is a Leeds scheme which embraces two pro-jects, one targeted at the 17–20 year-old age group. Both projects make extensive use of voluntary workers. The probation office finds volunteers in the community and when the court makes probation orders, the probation officer and project volunteers help the boys to sort out their problems. The boys mostly live at hotels or day centres. The Probation Service considers intensive probation too tentative.

55

The boys, however, are delighted with the whole idea. Over a period of six to eight weeks, the workers give them individual attention, talk to them, ask them why they keep offending and so on. There is a lot of wickedness about. Some of them have grown up surrounded by it for ten to fifteen years. If you are hoping to turn them round and stop them being criminals – it just can't be done. That drives you back to ask: What is the purpose of the law and sentencing? The main purpose is punishment and rehabilitation. They can be helped more effectively in the community.

LL: On the whole community care covered a longer period – say, three years. When I think of intensive supervision, I think of going to a centre.

MT: Everybody would agree that if a person is dangerous, he should be locked up. But the difficulty is to tell who is dangerous. Quite a lot of rape victims are women who have been subjected to forced intercourse with an ex-lover.

LL: You stick to the idea that when you break the law you must see it in terms of punishment?

MT: I wish the Probation Service could say that. Until they do, the judiciary will go on sentencing people to prison. You have to understand that prison is for training, but probation is also for punishment. It is a continuum.

LL: You said that young offenders under 18 should be sent to a government establishment, where we presume that the staff are qualified.

MT: It is thought that should they go into the child care system.

LL: Would you say that nobody under 18 should be put into the prison system?

MT: Between 16 and 18, it should be for the judge to decide. Some 17-year-olds are still children.

LL: So for one reason or another, you would keep them out of the prison system?

MT: The only problems are the financial ones of setting up the regional secure units, because of the security. If someone is expected to reoffend, they should be put into prison.

LL: Nobody under 16 should be in custody.

MT: From 16 to 18, I think ideally there should be a choice. Most young offenders, I strongly believe, are better and more safely looked after in the community. I would have a lot fewer in custody. The ones in custody are the ones I would have reason to believe are dangerous. Keep prison for the dangerous. Those who are in prison should be in community prisons. One of the problems with Feltham is that it has far too large a catchment area. The young want to be near their family and friends and be able to have visitors. Feltham does not deal with bullying. The shift system is not good, but prison officers will not go for more flexibility. The supervision is not nearly good enough. The psychiatric department there is up in arms. The Governor means well, but the staff are very bolshie. Feltham is too full. The real problem is the Prison Officers' Association. They never really accepted Fresh Start. That is why I am all for privatization.

LL: I think the idea of privatization is disgusting.

MT: The prison system started to go wrong when it was nationalized in the 1870s. Certainly nobody is going to make much money out of running British prisons, but it is a useful tracking exercise. All prisons are run either for the inmates or the officers; it is the function of the State to see that they are run for the prisoners, and not for the officers. Some prisons, like Dartmoor and Feltham, are under the control of the officers.

LL: It is not much of a life being a prison officer.

MT: But because it is not much of a life, they will arrange the rotas so that they are looking after the Alsation dogs or sitting in the offices. In spite of the huge ratio of staff, there will be nobody on the landings. It is a game really. I don't want to say that I have no confidence in prison officers. They do well, and things vary very much from establishment to establishment. But when you have got into a really bad situation, you have to break it. It is management's ability to manage, without absolute security of tenure. Privatizing prisons is a way of making things subject to contract.

LL: To get back to young offenders. What is the thinking behind intensive probation?

MT: The kind of boys who commit most crime perhaps have no home, living in squats, no job, existing on alcohol, getting into the habit of robbery and so on. You get them in court, you send them off to an establishment, you keep them there, and when they are eventually released they are worse than when they went in. Instead of keeping them locked up for two or three years, under our intensive probation scheme we promise them very intensive help – teach them to read and write, start to educate them. These boys really love it. They begin to learn that it is possible to live in a different way

57

altogether. Nobody had ever really taken the trouble to help them before. There is no evidence yet as to what the rehabilitation rate is. Even if it is just the same as for prison, at least intensive probation is cheaper.

LL: I welcome punishment and care in the community. What I want to get down to is the practical problem of life in the community – life for a boy who comes from a bad home.

MT: I don't think we will always succeed. The Criminal Justice Act only comes into force this autumn [1992], and we ought to give the CJA and the new sentencing patterns, as well as the many changes in the Probation Service, a chance. They are the best way to deal with young offenders. They are being carefully researched. Let us see in three to five years' time. What could go wrong is a sudden whoosh of punitiveness by the general public. There is not much difference between locking them up in prison and locking them up in regional secure units.

LL: If you are going to have intensive probation, is six or eight weeks enough?

MT: I think the pattern should be: if you have two years' probation, you start off with two months' intensive probation at the beginning and you follow up with careful monitoring. Every boy should have a father-figure. The Probation Service are the experts in dealing with young offenders – much better than Feltham.

LL: When you talk about people living in the community, you are assuming that they are going to live at home?

MT: You find them a hostel or cheap lodgings. They will certainly not all have families. In the end they have to live with good families. You have got to try to teach them *how* to live.

LL: One other point – you did mention that some are dangerous so far as we can judge. You would not want them to live at home?

MT: I have had a lot of research about boys who have committed rape – rape by boys of 15 who have raped girls of 15. You cannot let them back into the community. These boys have not got the faintest idea of how to live and how to treat women. You have got to teach them.

Sarah Curtis

Chairman of a Youth Court

Mrs Sarah Curtis was appointed a Juvenile Court Magistrate in 1978 and became Chairman of an Inner London Bench three years later. She has been Chairman in the Islington area, and in Kensington and Chelsea. She has also sat on the Lord Chancellor's committee for the selection of magistrates. A journalist by profession, specializing in social and education issues, she published *Juvenile Offending – Prevention through Intermediate Treatment* in 1989.

LORD LONGFORD: Should different principles be applied to young offenders?

SARAH CURTIS: Yes, and this is enshrined in statute. In the Juvenile Court we have to have regard to the welfare of the child. A year ago, the implementation of the 1989 Children Act put the care jurisdiction of Juvenile Courts into new Family Courts. I am a Chairman in the Family Courts as well. This covers children under 18 who need protection, and adults sorting out divorce, maintenance and so on. For the first time I am meeting competent people sorting out their lives.

LL: What about offenders to the age of 21?

SC: I stop at 16 and from next month 17.

LL: Are the young people responding?

SC: Yes – most are being turned round and given support, interest and change to enable them to accelerate the process of growing out of crime. Most young people will grow out of crime, figures suggest that. I'm more interventionist, though; I believe we can create conditions for people to learn to live in proper social relations with other people.

LL: You mean outside penal custody?

SC: I don't see how anyone could send a young person to custody for repeated theft. There's no point. Penal custody is fortunately almost in the past – except for 17-year-olds. The reason why custody has been reduced in the last decade is that two things have happened: first, there's been the recognition that locking them up was pretty useless – the rate of reoffending was too high; secondly, there is now better provision of alternatives to custody in heavy-end schemes that really do confront young people with what they've been doing and give them opportunities to do other things. The '83 government gave the pump-priming money for voluntary organizations to set up alternatives. These have been very effective, though they are patchy and a major fault in the present juvenile system is that it depends on where you live as to what you get. There are still some areas where there's hardly a youth club. But on the whole, these are the reasons why things have improved.

LL: So you would give credit to Juvenile Court Magistrates and social workers?

SC: In alliance. There have been really good examples of the court, social workers, education and the police working together. It only works where there are sufficient places for kids and parents to be involved in support groups – helping parents to control their children. Young people should take responsibility for themselves.

LL: Do you call them by their first names?

SC: Yes, always. When counsel forget and refer to Mr — – and they are nearly always male – we remind them. This is part of the skill needed now. There needs to be a dialogue between child, parent, officers – everyone needs to be drawn in.

LL: What about intermediate treatment?

SC: All districts should have schemes for persistent thieves to get a Youth Training Scheme or youth employment, but some don't. It is clear what needs to be done, but there is a lack of resources. They are not properly spread. After-school play schemes and youth clubs are needed which are not regimented. You need supervision for those on the fringes of offending and other schemes for those deep in crime. You need schemes that will occupy most of their time because they're often likely to be expelled or suspended from school.

LL: And even if they get a job, that limits how much remedial treatment they get?

SC: Most can't get jobs, especially the unskilled. If you can motivate them to go on training courses, resources are essential.

LL: Through grants to voluntary bodies or local authorities?

SC: But they've had tremendous cutbacks. All local authorities are besieged with campaigns for old people to have domiciliary help – everyone's crying out. But it is vital that young people are enabled to live ordinary lives.

LL: If the Prime Minister asked you to give some advice, what would you say?

SC: That every local authority should have to put forward a plan for preventing juvenile offending through a complementary spread of resources from after-school activities to intermediate treatment, fully funded so that the needs of every kind of young person can be met.

LL: I am told that out of nine IT centres in Lambeth, only one is dealing with youth.

SC: That's another muddle in intermediate treatment; it covers so many aspects.

LL: So each local authority should draw up plans on how to deal with youngsters in trouble. Who should authorize these plans?

SC: It's now split between the Home Secretary and the Department of Health. The preventive side is down to the Department of Health; the Home Office is where police come in. The police are a very important factor – in some areas they're vital to the sifting of people going to court.

LL: And you would try to prevent children going to custody?

SC: The big fall in custody has happened since the boost of some resources in '83, which gave more options to Juvenile Courts. Magistrates have seen that these are marginally more effective than custody. We've still to convince everyone that you don't learn to be a good citizen in a day. Look at how long it takes a child to read! People won't learn a sense of morality and social responsibility in a day, particularly those brought up in extremely difficult circumstances who have often witnessed violence and are very poor. Poverty is a very important factor.

LL: For those coming from bad homes, are you going to send them back there?

61

sc: Yes, if they can be helped to see what else there is in their neighbourhood and some support is given to the parents. Very few parents actually set their children into crime. What they cannot give their children, because they themselves never received it, is nurturing; they don't know how to pay attention to kids or play with them and be what a parent is. If their parental skills can be reinforced, it will much better for the children to return. But parenting-skill support often isn't there. The trick is to divert people from offending when they are younger. Taking them away from home is pretty useless because they have to return eventually.

The trend has been to encourage everybody to integrate into community. I think this is right.

ll: So you have no criticism of current legislation except for a lack of resources?

sc: Legislation has improved all the time, but laws are only a tool to enable problem-solving – they don't solve the problems themselves. The primary need is for resources for suitable alternatives in the community.

ll: Some penal reformers are worried that bringing the 17-year-olds into Youth Courts may spread resources too thinly for them and for the 16-year-olds.

sc: You can be very mature at 16 or very immature at 17. There isn't the same provision for 17-year-olds as there is for 16-year-olds, and as resources are stretched for the 16s there'll be even less for the 17s. Most boroughs will take 17-year-olds into IT; the 17s are bigger and tougher but there is no sign of extra people with extra training to cope. They do need more resources and the teaching of more skills.

ll: What about the respective roles of the social and probation services?

sc: Community service is not much use – offenders need a degree of maturity to get any benefit there. Community service and probation orders are now to be combined – if they're capable of community service, they are likely to be OK anyway.

ll: Would your court deal with very serious offenders?

sc: No. Murder and rape cases would go straight to a higher court. We deal with much less serious cases than adult courts. We can send anyone to six months' youth custody; for violence, we can go up to a year, if there is more than one count. Everything non-violent, we have enough powers to deal with.

In the ten or twelve years that I've been a magistrate, I have only twice been in a position to send someone to penal custody. There should be other ways for younger children, of course. Now, all we can do is give them a conditional discharge which means that if they don't offend again in twelve months, that's the end of it. We can fine the parents, or them; occasionally we can send them to attendance centres or place them under supervision. The best kind of intervention would be to remove them entirely from the criminal scene. Some people argue that the shock of going to court is enough to bring them up with a start.

LL: Keeping them away from court is a negative, isn't it?

SC: It would mean adjusting the law. If a child is under a supervision order, that means keeping appointments with your supervisor. It is part of the supervisor's skill and tact to introduce some support. It depends on your social worker. I think that all social workers should have three years of proper training, not the two as now. Probation officers the same. I don't see how you can be equipped for extremely onerous responsibilities with only two years' training. Magistrates are saying, 'She's only a young social worker; they have no experience, they don't know.'

LL: How far do you check up on the results of IT?

SC: I advocate that intermediate treatment centres should send reports to magistrates of how the young people fared. There should be feedback, both to encourage magistrates and to give them a quality-marker. As it is, we only hear if they break the terms of the supervision order.

Judge Mark Dyer
Circuit Judge

His Honour Judge Mark Dyer was President of the Council of HM Circuit Judges in 1992. He has been a Crown Court Recorder, Liaison Judge for the County of Wiltshire, a member of the Judicial Studies Board and is now a member of the Parole Board.

LORD LONGFORD: Do you approve of the general trends in sentencing over the last ten years whereby fewer young people are sent to prison?

MARK DYER: First of all, I was sad that Borstal training died. As an idea, it seemed there was a lot going for it. If you deprive a young man of liberty, the worst thing is to do nothing with him. To have an idle regime leads to bullying and the rise of a subculture. If any regime takes away liberty, you need to substitute hard work, perhaps education. They should go out better than when they came in, even if it is only to be literate and numerate. That will help them get employment. The sad thing is that too much time in young offender institutions seems to be wasted. The more money you spend, the more people you employ in training, the better things are.

LL: So you agree with recent trends?

MD: The recent trend of avoiding sending offenders to youth custody is good, and – quite contrary to popular belief – judges are enthusiastic about avoiding custody. I have worked with the Probation Service, helped set up new teams for the probation system and started various sorts of community service projects. The vital thing is not to waste time: a project to challenge these youngsters will make them come out better. In Wiltshire, we have an extremely good community project in Swindon where they run a scheme for mentally handicapped children. It is an all-day Saturday club which interests a high proportion of young thugs, if I can call them that, to such an extent that when they have completed their community service hours, many return voluntarily to meet people worse off than themselves.

LL: The worst offenders can improve when someone worse off comes into their life.

MD: Some said they couldn't bear it. If young offenders benefit from it, that's magnificent. For the hard core – those to whom you've said, 'If you return to me for breaching the community service order, there'll be no alternative to custody' – it is the only sanction left.

LL: But often community service work is not available?

MD: London is very short of suitable community service projects.

LL: Is the 1991 Criminal Justice Act making a difference to sentencing practice?

MD: Not a great deal of difference for young offenders – things were going that way anyway. Older offenders? Well, there are real criticisms about the Act. The idea that you're not allowed to take into account more than one previous conviction when sentencing an offender may make it appear harder to send people to prison – but it could have quite a different effect, namely more contested cases where the prosecuting authorities will wait for two counts. The judge will then have the right to send that person to prison.

LL: Will the 1991 Act reduce the numbers in prison?

MD: There won't be a lack of co-operation from judges whether they approve of the legislation or not. It is not easy in practice – I have met criminologists who think that the new ideas are virtually unworkable. Not taking into account the fact that a man has committed the offence before is an absurdity. Then in the new Act you get a switch-over if the offence concerns sex or violence – a longer sentence commensurate with previous sex or violent crimes.

LL: Will the Act affect current sentencing policy?

MD: Each case will be judged on its merits, to try to keep young people out of custody.

LL: Do you feel that public opinion has changed as regards young people getting lighter treatment?

MD: Some young people commit the most horrific crimes. There must be some secure establishments for the safety of the public. It's hard now for judges to see people of 16 and 17 committing ruthless burglaries, with bloodshed at times, and being unable to restrain them. I agree with requirements to improve the care of these young people – there should be a proper, humane regime – but young offenders just end up laughing at you if all you say is, 'Try another community project.'

LL: But where do you send these people? To local government secure units? Would you agree that a national plan should be drawn up?

MD: Completely. It's absurd that there isn't a proper, efficient system of care and education for the young offender. This should have been done years ago. But the law isn't the only profession to fail in this: subnormal people who commit shoplifting – there's nowhere to send them, either. One of my most painful cases was a 16-year-old girl who went shoplifting – mentally subnormal parents, just repetitive conditioning. Such cases should not to go custody but the court has few alternatives.

LL: Yes, but wouldn't local government secure units be better?

MD: But judges don't want to be faced with these terrible dilemmas. The main means of prevention is detection. If enough efficient policing is available for detection to be high, crime will fall. Is it just lack of resources? There seems to be no improvement in clear-up rates. And now that prosecutions are in the hands of the Crown Prosecution Service, the police tend to lose interest in the case. Also, training in giving evidence is essential. It's the jury the police have to convince, and the police can look clowns with good defence lawyers.

LL: Some feel that the right of silence should be modified.

MD: The right of silence should be there, but juries should be told when a defendant has exercised it.

Old-style judges will be around for a time yet, but the general feeling among Circuit Judges is to give a fair trial and a sound but not too long sentence. It is important that there are now to be appeals both ways. The effect has not been fully understood – it will be on the judge's mind that a too lenient sentence can be challenged. It's easy to say that judges are over-severe. It can go a little too far the other way.

What we need is a good institution either through central government or local authorities. Young offenders should not be sent to adult prisons, with these suicides of youths in senior prisons. The sex offenders are very prone to bullying, lack of self-esteem. Money must be provided, and trained staff.

But it all comes back to trying to keep them out of these places. A really good Probation Service could be the best protection the public could have.

LL: When you are going to sentence a 15-year-old, how do you know what to do with him?

MD: There needs to be a full probation officer's report covering the options and discussing the various alternatives. The judges will then ask the Probation Service where this person should go. They will suggest the place. Much trouble is taken.

LL: Should a line be drawn to keep people under 21 out of custody – 18, 17, when?

MD: If at all possible, we should prevent the 14s and 15s going to prison. Psychologically damaging – and the others can be cruel to them.

II
Social
Organizations

Dr Michael Little

Dartington Social Research Unit

Dr Michael Little was educated at Liverpool Collegiate School and Birmingham University. He took his Ph.D at Oxford University on the subject of young men in prison (now published as a book in an abbreviated form). He has been working for the last ten years at the Dartington Social Research Unit on Social Policy, which is a part of Bristol University, though not located in Bristol. The Research Unit is a Department of Health designated Child Care Unit, and the Department provides most of the funding.

LORD LONGFORD: This word 'child' is a curious one, when you see these strapping young people being referred to as children—

MICHAEL LITTLE: It has always struck me as being one of the nice things about the Department of Health that they treat somebody under the age of 18 as a child, which to all intents and purposes they are. The Home Office tend to treat them as difficult young adults.

LL: They are called young adults, aren't they?

ML: We tend to call them children up to 18; we also call them young people.

LL: It is an interesting issue, this question of how you see them.

ML: You get quite interesting comparisons in the philosophies which underpin the different pieces of legislation by different departments. Parental responsibility underpins the Children Act of 1989, which is trying to help parents wherever possible to parent their own children. There is also the idea that parents should share care where necessary with the State. That contrasts markedly with parental

71

responsibility as expressed in the new Criminal Justice Act, which is about making parents pay when their children do wrong. These two pieces of legislation have been pushed through at the same time.

LL: Would you say that in the last ten years you have been working on all forms of offender?

ML: All forms, from the very minor, petty offender right through to the most serious offenders.

LL: How have attitudes changed with regard to the treatment of young offenders?

ML: In the last 30 years there have been major differences in the care, treatment and general interventions with the very young offender – those aged between 10 and 14 years. Thirty years ago, the Mary Bell case – she was convicted of murder when she was just 9 or 10 – led to the opening of the youth treatment centres, in which we were involved.

LL: That has all been to the good, has it?

ML: Yes. Thirty years ago there were some 18,000 young people living in residential approved schools – reformatory schools up and down the country, established in Victorian times. They took the youngest offenders and their contribution to their life history was almost entirely negative—

LL: Just a moment – I suppose one might find somebody in these places who was very good?

ML: Yes, I am sure you could. But it strikes me that young offenders between 10 and 14 will benefit from a lot of diversions to keep them out of the criminal justice system. They are likely to benefit from some form of benign treatment which keeps them at home living with their parents.

LL: You wouldn't move them from a bad home?

ML: Only when that is necessary. And if they are severely disturbed, i.e. their behaviour is extreme and their pathology is much more than simple delinquency, then they are likely to get a very well-considered, thought-out intervention, removing the child from home into specialist foster care, or residential care.

LL: Wait a bit. You say that is happening now?

ML: We are talking about 10–14 year-olds, so they would most likely go into some form of foster care.

72

LL: So foster care is a new development?

ML: Foster care is not a new development – it is really moving young people out of these old residential centres into the community. That is the great step forward. I would say the effort ought to be made to replicate, wherever possible, the advances made for the younger offender – to apply them to the older adolescent offender up to 21.

LL: All the way up?

ML: Yes. I have met many young offenders up to the age of 21 and they have never struck me as being – despite all the bravado and machismo – adults in every sense of the word. They need support, they need help.

LL: I am quite sure of that.

ML: The difficult area we get into is the question of the victim and punishment. It *is* very important that victims of crime should get some kind of support and should also feel that they get just deserts from the legal and justice systems. Currently, they often feel very distanced from both systems. Another problem is that attempts to punish offenders often only tend to prolong or exacerbate a criminal career.

LL: Are you saying that we should not send these people to prison? Take these young people at Feltham, do you think they should not be there, or most of them? I am not talking only about the under-18s. If you take them right up to 21 – are you saying that they should not be sent to penal custody? What about when they have committed rape or murder? There may be only a small number, but you couldn't say they all ought to be out and about.

ML: There are a small number of young people who, for their own protection or because society needs to be protected, should be locked up. It depends on how far you want to take this. I would not necessarily feel that youth custody is the right place to lock up somebody, whatever their crime.

LL: Yes, but we have to look at what we want a few years from now, without being totally unrealistic. Social reforms are, after all, brought about by people who do look ahead.

ML: Well, 30 years ago the most difficult young people would have gone into some form of residential care, large residential institutions with some form of secure accommodation, or more likely into the Prison Department custody system. Now we estimate that at any one time there are about 150 children of between 10 and 18 years of age who need to be in secure accommodation. At the moment half of them are in youth custody and half in places like Aycliffe, St Charles and Glenthorne. At great expense, the Department of Health have opened these two youth treatment centres. They are also prepared to pay high prices at specialist institutions like Aycliffe, and that shelters about half of the most difficult young people in the country.

LL: Say about 120 in Aycliffe and 30 in St Charles—

ML: Another 40 in Glenthorne – about 200 in all. Only a very small proportion, say 15 to 20, are extremely difficult.

LL: What are you going to do with these young people? Take the population at Feltham, 800, two-thirds of them on remand. Where would you send them all?

ML: You would have to try to develop very imaginative schemes to cut short the criminal career so that, over time, the numbers entering places like Feltham or the other young offender institutions would reduce markedly.

LL: So you do want to reduce numbers markedly.

ML: We ought to be trying to get down to a core of violent young people who need some kind of training. They obviously need to be contained, but there are not very many young people in the country who need to be locked up. Their violence may not be physical, but consist of driving a car at lunatic speeds. Obviously these ones do need to be locked up.

LL: Well, well, that could be the saying of the week.

ML: Locking young people up has all kinds of other functions for society.

LL: Do you know the work of Andrew Rutherford? He is very much on that line. Perhaps you agree with him.

ML: I do, except that he tends to say that young people will grow out of crime, which of course they probably will. But I think they need a lot of help to grow out of crime. One of the depressing aspects of seeing young people in custody is how entrenched they become in a criminal career. They see themselves as criminals; they enjoy the identity. They enjoy people seeing them as tough nuts and difficult to deal with. They see themselves as being older than they actually are. They use criminal language which they probably do not understand. But that tells you something about them. It tells you

74

that this life-style offers them something which they probably could not get elsewhere.

Now that means that if you want change, you have got to work quite hard with them. There are two ways of going about it: you can either stop the identity developing – keep them off their criminal career – or, once they are in, try very hard to channel their—

LL: We are still left with the question: what do you do with these people? A large proportion have got very bad homes. I mean, a weekly visit to a probation officer – you are not suggesting that is good enough?

ML: No. But you have to be careful here. There are different types of criminal career. Some young offenders are petty offenders – they just steal Mars Bars or run away with other people's bicycles. They don't cause us very much concern at all and they do grow out of crime quite quickly. Other people become what we call persistent delinquents. They get convicted two or three times in court, and their long-term turn-out is very poor indeed.

LL: But what if you want to keep people out of penal custody? Custody is a very ambiguous word because, after all, a local secure unit is custody and Aycliffe would appear to be custody.

ML: Well, of course, if it were me, I would much prefer to be in Aycliffe than in a young offender institution. There is a qualitative difference – better staff ratio, the ambience is better.

LL: That is very important.

ML: Another aspect of this is that young people who are locked up in youth treatment centres or local authority secure units are not necessarily locked up for the period of time they are there. They have visits home and outside distractions of various kinds. The Aycliffe, St Charles and Glenthorne experience is far preferable and the outcome is very much better. We have found that serious offenders placed in youth treatment centres, not in youth custody, and particularly with some kind of intervention which looks into their family life – those are the ones who do best in the long run.

LL: Let us go back to the philosophical side of all this. Do you think there is something in the penal approach which is different from the caring approach? One is punishment. But sick people need treatment, don't they?

ML: Yes, there are people who need protection; they need support. They are people who require the best professional help we can find for them, wherever possible. You don't always get that in the prison system. And if you look at it from the young person's point of view, their experience of prison is usually, of course, not Feltham, which isn't too bad by Prison Department standards. Their first experience is usually one of the big dispersal prisons, like Birmingham or Dorchester, where you are remanded with three others in a cell waiting for your weekly court case. That is your first experience of prison. If later you are moved on to Feltham, which the Prison Department see as one of the more benign institutions, you are lucky.

LL: Does the future lie in treating these young people as though they were still at school?

ML: We feel so, yes. But we have to be careful here. One of the failings, we feel, of the youth treatment centres, and certainly of Aycliffe, is that all the attention is placed on the young person's offence and they tend therefore to miss certain other key aspects of the young person's career.

LL: They have a good mix at Aycliffe – educationalists, psychologists, nurses, probation officers, ex-prison officers. What are you objecting to?

ML: Over one-third of the staff employed at Aycliffe are probably ex-teachers. But out of 300 or so youth-treatment-type children we have looked into, I think between them they have managed to get a handful of O levels, a handful of qualifications; and out of that 300 only half have managed to get a job. Of those who got a job, half of them left the job within three days, because they did not have the social skills to hold it down. They just could not cope and walked out, never to return to work again.

Aycliffe will help to keep them from reoffending, they are much better equipped. If a dangerous situation occurs they won't attack somebody – but they can't work. Now what does that say about their future life chances? The difficulty is that in the care system education is not greatly valued. In English society, care situations have evolved separately from education, whereas on the Continent, under the pedagogic system, care situations are part of education. The Department of Education never talk to the Department of Health and education departments do not talk to local authority social service departments, so there is a great divide there.

Actually, we have found that long-term prisoners – those who are locked up for four years or more – do better educationally in the prison system than they do in the local authority or youth treatment centre system. The reason is that the youth custody situations tend to be more pragmatic. One young man, for example, a murderer,

76

went to a youth treatment centre and subsequently to a youth custody centre, where he was taught to drive. At the youth treatment centre it never crossed their minds to teach him to drive. Many of those going into Prison Department custody get degrees through the Open University.

LL: The young people?

ML: We are talking about those who stay. Some of the young people we followed up had been to youth treatment centres.

LL: The people you are talking about have been in prison several years?

ML: Andrew Rutherford says they grow out of crime. They will, but they have got to have something for when they do grow out of it. If they have got a qualification, or if they have an interest in rugby, they have got something tangible. If they haven't got anything for afterwards, they end up becoming homeless. The saddest cases we come across are not the persistent delinquents who go on through the prison system, they are the offenders who become homeless, who grow out of crime but really have no relationships with anybody at all. One almost wishes they would reoffend, so they would get into some system or other.

LL: What are you going to do about all the young people who quarrel with their families and become homeless?

ML: The answer would be very much the answer we have given with regard to the Children Act. For many years the effort was made to rescue children from their awful families, and the numbers in care shot up. But then, of course, we discovered that they were no better off because the State does not make good parents. Then preventive measures came in and the numbers went down. But it should not be either one thing or the other. The idea under the Children Act is to encourage parental responsibility, to help them to parent their own children through shared-care methods; wherever possible to keep the child at home. For example, we think now that the incidence of child sexual abuse is 6 per cent. Not all the authorities agree with us, but we think it is 6 per cent.

LL: Do you really think you can get at the truth of a matter like that?

ML: We feel it is about 6 per cent. The number of children who come to be looked after by the State at any time during childhood is less than 2 per cent. We don't have the capacity to rescue that number – 6 per cent – so a lot of disadvantaged children have to

77

remain at home, in whatever context. The other aspect is that in the long run most young people go back home. If they have been in local authority care, if they have been in youth custody, if they have been in a youth treatment centre, most of them go back home. Not always because it is the best place for them, but because when *we* have all given up, when we have gone home, when you are 20, 21, 22, home is the place you go to.

LL: The ones I have seen, the ones in Soho, they have not gone home.

ML: We have just written a study called *Return*, which is about the experience of children separated into State care. Now 87 per cent of those children eventually return to live with their parents, or other relatives. Out of those who have had youth treatment, over 60 per cent eventually return to live with their parents or other relatives. That tells us an awful amount about how important the family is. At home there is always a bed for them; home is a bolt-hole.

LL: If you have a lot of young people who ought not to be in penal custody, would you really try to leave them at home? There is a scheme, I believe, for probation officers to visit people in their homes, a more intensive form of probation. Do you think there is any future in that?

ML: I feel sure there have been some successful steps forward for the younger offender. It means, first of all, diversion – keeping them out of the system. I would do absolutely nothing in those cases.

LL: But you can't keep on cautioning them, if they go on stealing.

ML: You can caution them three or four times, if it stops them getting into the prison system. In many cases it keeps them from reoffending.

LL: Those I spoke to at Feltham said they had benefited from being there. They can have some therapy there. You don't think these young offenders need positive therapy?

ML: I am sure some young people at Feltham would benefit.

LL: You can't just leave them in a bad home.

ML: Most of them don't need therapy. First of all I would do nothing at all. Then I would have a caution. Then I would have some supervision, where somebody visited the young person at home. If necessary, I would provide some respite care, letting the young person leave home for short periods in a residential setting or in

78

some kind of foster-care setting. If absolutely necessary, I would remove the young person for prolonged periods—

LL: To some sort of children's home?

ML: Yes, some sort of open children's home with professionals, who know about young people. I would try all of these things – attendance centres always interest me. On the face of it, it's hard to imagine what they offer the young person. You go along, you spend your Saturday afternoon with a policeman, playing ping-pong. But it is another intervention. It keeps them out of the custody system a little bit longer. That is often enough to pay off. Community service, eventually – punishment in the community, if that is what you want to call it. All these things are positive in the sense that the longer you can keep them out of the custody system, the better your long-term chances are, even if it does mean keeping them with their family.

LL: When you say 'keep them out', you mean preventing them going to local authority secure units?

ML: If possible – for as long as possible, yes.

LL: You believe in the family?

ML: Yes. I do believe in the family, but not in the sort of ideal family type. Most of these people live in very dislocated families. They might have single mothers, they might live with their grandparents, or they might shift from one divorced partner to another. It is not the ideal type, but it is in the end the one continuous thing that will exist for these young people, regardless of whatever we do. Whether we lock them up for years, whether we birch them – that is the one thing you can say will be on the scene.

LL: Is it oversimplifying it to say that you see collaboration between the social services and the family as the way forward?

ML: Yes, some kind of shared care between the State and the family.

LL: Not just taking away from the family?

ML: No. Some kind of realistic assessment of how that family functions.

I would like to make just two further points, one of which I consider to be most important. There is one thing that could be done in the short term to help the system more than anything else, and that is to provide good alternatives to remands to custody, as opposed to sentences to custody. Most experiences of custody for young people are, in fact, short-term remands in the most awful conditions in the big prisons – locked up for 23 hours a day, overcrowding and so on. That starts them off on a criminal career.

LL: Are you saying that they should not be in custody at all, or that there ought to be better conditions?

ML: The great majority of those young people could be sheltered outside custody.

LL: What do you call 'sheltered' – bail hostels, that sort of thing?

ML: There are good bail support schemes; there are imaginative probation schemes with very close supervision of the young person at home; there are foster-parent schemes, where the foster-parents look after the young person, enough to quieten them down. There are good local authority remand places. Remand is very important. The reason I say that is that most of the young people I refer to in my book *Young Men in Prison* were never eventually convicted – never found guilty.

The other dimension is that many of the young people we found successfully leaving youth treatment centres then get involved in petty crime, are remanded in custody and are separated from their homes where they may have made some progress. If they have developed a new relationship, that is wrecked. If they have managed to get themselves a job, they lose the job. And if they have managed to get themselves on to an education scheme, they lose the education opportunity. Remand wrecks their lives and they are almost back to square one.

LL: To put it crudely – much more generous grant of bail?

ML: Yes, that or specialist foster schemes.

LL: There are such things? Would people foster somebody for a few weeks?

ML: Barnardo's do that. The National Children's Homes have an imaginative scheme in Hampshire.

My second point is that when we went to Aycliffe, they said: 'We have all these extremely difficult children, we are the largest centre for difficult children in Europe.' We found that about 20 of their residents were extremely difficult and disturbed; 40 extremely difficult, needing some kind of specialist intervention, and the rest should not have been there at all.

Now, in the North-East there are far more residential beds than in London, where there are not many beds available for these young people. We found that at the age of 11 a lot of young people in the North-East received a care order for delinquency and went into a

Community Home with Education. These are the old reformatory schools which still exist up there. They run away at 12 because they don't like it, and the local authority send them to Aycliffe. At Aycliffe they go into assessment and are recommended for a treatment period in secure accommodation. They leave at 13, go home and at 14 reoffend. The magistrates see that they have already been to Aycliffe and make an order for youth custody. They get out, reoffend and at 15 end up back at Aycliffe.

Well now, that same young person in London, at the age of 11 after a first offence, would be cautioned. They would probably be cautioned several more times between 12 and 13. But at 14, if they offend perhaps for the fourth time, they would receive an attendance centre order. At 16, they end up in youth custody. But during that period they have been kept out of any form of residential care or secure youth custody. The system in the North is very different from that in the South.

Andrew Rutherford

Chairman of the Howard League for Penal Reform

Andrew Rutherford has been Chairman of the Howard League since 1984 and is a Reader in Law at Southampton University. He left the prison service in 1973, later becoming Deputy Governor of Everthorpe Juvenile Young Offender Unit. He is the author of three books: *Growing out of Crime* (1986; reissued in 1992 with two additional chapters), *Prisons and the Process of Justice* (1984), and *Criminal Justice and the Pursuit of Decency* (to be published in 1993).

LORD LONGFORD: I will begin by quoting the opening sentences of the Preface to your book *Growing out of Crime*:

If a young person becomes involved in crime or other troublesome behaviour, it is tempting to parents or teachers to imagine that the responsibility and solution lie elsewhere. By creating a network of criminal justice, welfare and mental health arrangements, public policy holds out the seductive offer of an institutional fix; although the offer may be appealing, it is not an answer. If young people are to grow out of troublesome behaviour, the home, school and other developmental institutions must be encouraged and equipped to hold on during difficult and sometimes volatile phases. Formal intervention carries the threat of exile from a normal environment and the consequently inevitable waste of a chance for normal growth and development. Existing policy trends must be reversed, so as to direct attention to the everyday and intuitive practice which holds the most promise.

And the last paragraph of your final chapter, in which you say:

The overriding need is for public policy to take full account of good existing practice. In other words, there has to be recognition by policy-makers that

82

the most effective and least damaging work with young people in trouble occurs outside formal and specialized arrangements. It is informal and often intuitive action within the home and school that provides the best response to these young people. It is developmental institutions which quietly demonstrate that, above all else, what is needed is time.

Now, you are associated with the developmental approach. Did you invent this approach?

ANDREW RUTHERFORD: I don't think I invented it. I may have coined the term for the purposes of the book.

LL: In your Preface you reject all previous approaches pretty drastically – you are very bold.

AR: What I am really trying to argue is that intuitively good parents, schoolteachers and other people working with youngsters recognize that involvement in crime is likely to be transient. The problem with the previous interventions that I mention in my Preface is that they carry the danger of trapping the young person, rather than allowing him to move on.

LL: You propose to help these young people to develop without custody, and also – if I understand you rightly – without undue supervision. I want to pause on that question. You think custody is likely to do them more harm than good?

AR: I am absolutely convinced that custody for young people particularly is a very damaging experience. I think it is damaging for the young people themselves and, in the long run, it is damaging for society as a whole.

LL: How far do you object to custody provided by local authorities through their secure units? Have you the same objection?

AR: I would take an absolute position in keeping young people out of the prison system altogether.

LL: What about these local places? I have visited one or two. When you condemn custody, is that custody within the penal system, or that provided by local authorities?

AR: I am talking about young people under the age of 18 who have committed very serious offences, and in that situation the local authority would be responsible.

LL: Would you rather see them in local authority hands? Fully trained social workers are more caring than prison officers. If it has to be custody, you would rather it was under the local authority?

AR: Yes. The local authority are likely to provide a more sensitive degree of care for the young person, rather than the Prison Department. It strikes me as interesting that we have had a growing number of juveniles and other young people committing suicide in prison during the last two or three years. There has been none in local authority institutions, nor in the youth treatment centres.

LL: So if it has got to be custody, social workers are better than prison officers in the criminal justice system.

AR: I am not suggesting that there is not a great deal still to be done to improve the quality of treatment in the local authority centres.

LL: Coming back to the developmental theory – it is very challenging. How do you feel that you can apply it to young people who have broken the law? You obviously feel that good homes, good parents and good schooling take care of most young people. Nevertheless, there are quite a lot of them who misbehave and get expelled from school. The young people I meet at the New Horizon Youth Centre have nearly all quarrelled with their families. You get all categories of people who can't live at home.

AR: I am not arguing that I have some panacea for all the ills that beset young people, but in policy terms, if we take what we may call the developmental point of view as a signpost, the route is rather different from that if we go down the criminal justice road. In policy terms, you would need to put a massive investment of resources into supporting troubled families. I am really responding to your observation that a growing number of youngsters are running away from home, having fallen out with their families, drifting into London, living rough and getting into various sorts of trouble. As a society we would need to invest considerable resources to provide a variety of forms of support – I am not just talking about monetary support, but the kind of support that families themselves need to handle children who are giving parents a difficult ride. Although this would be very expensive, the cost of keeping youngsters in institutions is vastly greater than what I am proposing.

LL: Suppose an enlightened government came in and asked you what kind of support could be provided – what could it amount to?

AR: There are various little bits of experience to be taken into account. One example from the USA is the Head Start programme, a major effort by the Federal Government to put money into nursery and primary school education in the inner cities. That would be the

84

type of initiative. The best institutions for dealing with young persons in trouble are primarily home and schools.

LL: My trouble is that the young people I have seen have quarrelled with their homes. Good foster-homes are fine, but not easy to come by.

AR: Yes, indeed. I met somebody yesterday who was running a fostering programme, placing young people, 17–18 year-olds in trouble, with families – substitute families. Her difficulty is simply finding families. They are quite well paid, say £80 per week. I am convinced that if we were to put adequate resources into that sort of programme and into training the foster parents, much good would come of it.

LL: So that when you talk about supporting the home it might well be necessary to support an alternative school?

AR: The programme that I was told about yesterday concerned youngsters who stay in the foster-homes for five or six months – most of them have a history of care and have possibly appeared in court. The Crown Court arranges for them to go into the foster-homes.

LL: Courts do in fact sometimes arrange this?

AR: These are homeless youngsters, but instead of appearing in court with no fixed address, they go to court with foster-home arrangements already made. The scheme is funded through the National Children's Homes and Hampshire Probation Service. The money only allows for the young person to stay for five or six months. The experience of this particular project has been very encouraging. That brings me to the problem – in a sense it delays the crisis which comes after five months. Out they come and go back very often to the same pattern of life as before. In policy terms what is required is enough funding to give long-term support.

LL: Short of being in a home, are there no other options apart from custody or fostering?

AR: Many people in their early twenties are naturally moving out and setting up on their own. But if you have a history of care institutions behind you, that process is much more difficult. There may well be a need for foster-care support to extend well into somebody's twenties, so that they have a base and a person on whom they can rely.

LL: The difficulty is to find the foster-homes.

85

AR: The level of support provided to foster-parents may have to be improved. At the moment we only have a handful of schemes like this.

LL: You think fostering is better than any sort of institution?

AR: I am convinced of it, if proper resources are available. The cost at £80 per week is very much less expensive than in any institution.

LL: Some of these young delinquents have very bad records at school. What are the schools doing about it?

AR: Some of the educational requirements of the 1980s have not been particularly helpful in enhancing the pastoral responsibility of the schools themselves. They should have a policy of treating youngsters that extends beyond purely academic achievement. The danger of seeing that as the only important goal of the school is that it may well act to the disadvantage of those youngsters who require additional support. I am not unhappy about using the word 'welfare', in the nineteenth-century sense, if you like, of moving young people from their homes for their own good. But I do think that the school has the overriding responsibility for a youngster's welfare and this has been weakened by recent ideas in education and the pressures arising out of tables of excellence. The increased ease with which pupils can be expelled is also a problem.

Most of the children we are talking about are not usually from families who can help them from within their own resources. Jerry [Dr Jerome] Miller, who is a kind of moral crusader for children in trouble in the USA, will take delinquents at very short notice from the courts and find them a job to do within his busy office, staffed by professional people. I was there last year myself, working in the office, where there were three or four black youngsters who had been involved in the drug and robbery scene of Washington, DC. Also working in the office was a 55-year-old multimillionaire who had been involved in the production of pornographic material. The man lived in Oklahoma. Police raided his house and he faced a prison sentence. Miller's organization put an alternative plan to the court, offering to employ him and supervise him generally. Miller's organization is a voluntary body working with defence counsel on creative sentencing packages, or with jurors who decide on the question of punishment. Most of his funds come from wealthy clients.

LL: Is there a message for us there?

AR: I think so.

LL: What is the application?

AR: What it amounts to is that if you put the right package together it becomes much more difficult for the court to behave in a punitive and destructive way. Courts are mostly looking for a way to be constructive. There might be a long period of community service involved, but socially what you are trying to do is to respond sensitively to the offence. Since 1987, Miller has demonstrated that there is another way.

LL: I want to go on to the theory. There is a widespread acceptance of the idea that young people under 21 should not be treated as severely as adults. I suppose we would all agree we do not blame anyone so much if they are young.

AR: Full criminal responsibility in most societies is set at 18 years. I think it is partly to do with blame, but also a recognition that most, if not all, young people move on fairly naturally from crime; whereas that same notion of crime as a transient phase is less easy to apply in the case of an adult.

LL: When you get 18–19 year-olds, do you still say that they have got to be treated better in some way?

AR: I would argue that and give the present government some credit. Since 1988, public policy in terms of the Home Office and the excellent new Crown Prosecution Service has accepted this – that young adults should be cautioned. Courts are urged by various means by the Home Office and others to avoid custodial sentences wherever possible. This principle is becoming more widely accepted.

LL: The public accept the idea that young people grow out of crime and are not so much to blame. The prison population is going up in Britain, but while 47 per cent of offenders were under 21 in 1989, custodial sentences for young offenders have steadily gone down. We have been moving in two different directions.

AR: That is one of the paradoxes. Practice has led policy through the 1980s. Probation officers, prosecutors, magistrates and social workers have been imbued with an anti-prison ethos – now part of their occupational culture. Prisons are bad places and can't be made into good places. There is now absolute dissent from custody in the penal area. Magistrates are trying very hard to avoid it. But this same spirit of trying to find the most constructive way forward has not found ready acceptance in courts for adults.

LL: Due to public opinion. Do you think the developmental

approach should stop short at a certain point, or could it be played as a general principle of penal policy?

AR: I think it can be extended with regard to age range. There is no logical reason why it should stop at 21.

LL: Partly a question of growth. Do you associate the theory with the idea of maturity?

AR: It clearly loses its force as people get into their twenties. The last census showed that fewer young people of 18 had left home; many young people today are still at home in their twenties. I suppose that the developmental approach has a particular cogency for young people, but the underlying principle behind it is trying to seek the most constructive way forward – not denying the crime, but asking what we can do that won't make matters worse. How can we turn this bad situation into something that can be described as good?

LL: That is what the Howard League has always stood for?

AR: The League's position is not too distant from that held by perhaps the most far-seeing Home Secretary of the present century, Sir Winston Churchill, who said: 'There is a treasure in the heart of every person.'

At the time our interview took place, Andrew Rutherford had just published *Growing Out of Crime – the New Era*, a second edition of this important study. I shall turn to it briefly.

A note of triumph runs through the new chapters. The first edition of the book, he begins, was mostly written in 1984 against a background of considerable gloom and despair about dealing with young offenders in England and Wales. Over the years since then a dramatic change has taken place in the mood of juvenile justice practitioners. Their new confidence and optimism has arisen largely from a recognition of their own potential for shaping, rather than merely responding to, events. Above all else, they have been able to demonstrate that a strategy of minimal intervention is both feasible and effective. This transformation is all the more striking for having occurred during the 'Thatcher years', and it must be regarded as one of the most remarkable developments of post-war criminal justice. Rutherford seems convinced that the reduction in the use of custody has been accompanied by a diminution, or at any rate not an increase, in young offender crime.

In his last chapter Andrew Rutherford puts forward a number of proposals, all of them to be taken seriously. Two of them, however, clearly involve the injection of considerable sums of new money. The first is called 'Broad-Ranging Policies to Support the Home'. In Mr Rutherford's words, 'Related to the well-being of the home are a variety of policies encompassing housing, health and social services. Their common goal is to ease pressure on the parental task of bringing up children.' The second heading is 'Emphasis on the School's Pastoral Role'. In this case, 'There has to be a massive injection of resources into schools and other educational institutions, especially with respect to the strengthening of pastoral responsibilities.' We should all be with Andrew Rutherford on this.

Peter Thompson

Founder and Director of the Matthew Trust for Mental Patients and Victims of Crime

I have counted Peter Thompson a close friend for more than 30 years. He was the instigator of an inquiry called the Pakenham/Thompson Committee, with myself as chairman, which was set up as the result of Peter's experiences as an outpatient in a hospital's psychiatric department. The Committee's report paved the way for the establishment of a statutory inquiry into the problems of ex-offenders and ultimately to the establishment of the National Association for the Care and Resettlement of Offenders (NACRO).

Peter Thompson set up the Matthew Trust following his release from Broadmoor, where he spent four years (1965–9) detained under Section 65 of the Mental Health Act 1959. The Trust has concerned itself with the management of the treatment and disposal of patients in special hospitals and the mentally ill in prisons and at work.

LORD LONGFORD: You have done more for mentally disordered offenders than any other lay person. What about the younger ones – have you any special approach where they are concerned?

PETER THOMPSON: My particular concern, through the Matthew Trust, is the young offender who, prior to becoming an offender, was suffering from some kind of mental distress or mental disorder.

The first contact that the young offender has with the authorities or with the judicial system is, of course, through the police in terms of apprehension and initial detention. It is this stage, which is so vital to the eventual mental stability of the mentally ill offender, that has to be reassessed. Too often, young people who have committed what appears to be an intended antisocial offence are assumed by

90

the authorities to be straightforward young villains. Police doctors may be involved from time to time, but police doctors are seldom sufficiently trained or sufficiently alert to detect that the young offender before him is, in fact, mentally sick. Bear in mind the spirit of the 1983 Mental Health Act, which cautions us that had the person been well, the offence may not have been committed. Now, that spirit may not be reflected in the attitude and in the evaluation of the police doctor who sees the young person. The result is that the young boy or girl goes through the process from the police cell to the remand prison or secure unit undiagnosed as being mentally disturbed, and by implication receiving no treatment.

LL: Are you saying that, at the first stage when somebody has been arrested, there should be an improvement in the arrangements made?

PT: Not only in the arrangements, but the police doctor or police officer has little or no experience of psychiatric disorder.

LL: Are you saying that the police ought to have such experience?

PT: There are far too many; of course that would be impossible. Moreover, it would be impossible to call in a police doctor every time somebody is arrested. These two facts are the Achilles heel of the treatment of the young mentally sick person, because it is not until he or she reaches the court process, when the defence may introduce the mental health element, that the true nature of the situation becomes apparent. The defence can then ensure that a Mental Health order, rather than a punitive sentence, is passed. But, of course, up to the time of a formal defence in court, when his state of health is taken into account, the mentally ill young offender has possibly for several months been treated as a villain. During that time he has suffered an experience that he should never have been subjected to.

LL: Are you implying, therefore, that prison doctors should be better trained, or that different people should handle such cases?

PT: I can't use my own experience here—

LL: Why not? Bring it in.

PT: Well, I will, but I was not a young offender at the time. I was arrested – in fact, I surrendered, I gave myself up. I was put in a police cell and seen by a doctor who decided that I was not suffering from any mental disorder. He was only interested as to whether I had a cut or bruises and was not alert to anything else. I was then sent to Brixton Prison on remand, caged up with four others. There was no room to sit down. We were all waiting to be seen by the prison doctor, having had a shower. There were about 50 of us in all, in a network of wire cages. The doctor came about six o'clock in the evening and we were let out. A friendly prisoner said to me: 'He will ask you if you are depressed. You must say "yes" and you will be able to go into the prison hospital, where you can watch television.' I did so. No other questions were put to me, apart from the usual physical ones. But for that helpful tip-off I would have said 'no'. It would not have occurred to me to say otherwise.

LL: But you were depressed, weren't you?

PT: Yes, but you don't see it like that. Had I said 'no', I would have been locked up for 23 hours a day, for several months, like any other remand prisoner, though I was not a young offender in that sense. This experience is common, and is still common, and applies to young offenders. So even when you are put on remand, you have the police system and then the Prison Medical Service, which is not geared up to detecting whether somebody has a mental disorder.

LL: A very tricky issue. Is the implication that prison doctors ought to be better trained?

PT: Well, the police doctor and the prison doctor are the two medical specialists at different stages who should certainly be given better training in the basic means of diagnosis of mental disorder.

LL: Very difficult—

PT: The chances that you will see a police doctor are remote. It is very unlikely that when somebody is arrested in a high-profile case they will get the niceties of seeing a police doctor. Or that later the prison authorities will ask them, 'Are you depressed?' In the police mind and indeed in the prison management mind, the situation has been prejudged long before there has been an appearance in court.

Not all young offenders are subject, of course, to high-profile publicity, but when some local antisocial conduct has happened, the offence is likely to be stigmatized at the very beginning as having been committed by a rational villain. You have to open the minds of receiving officers in police cells and staff in remand prisons to the possibility that mental ill health is present. The partial solution is for police doctors and receiving officers in prisons to have a lay knowledge of the basic signals which might indicate a mental disorder. The trouble is those signals are not understood, because there is not sufficient lay knowledge. I say lay knowledge because, if you had to rely on them, there are not enough highly trained forensic psychiatrists available.

LL: When I was at Aycliffe, I met a senior staff member who had been bitten three times by an inmate, who went on biting people from the ages of 11 to 16, when he was moved on to a psychiatric nursing home. Are you saying that very disturbed young people like that should not be where they are now but in some other institution or hospital?

PT: That is too broad a question which I am not qualified to answer. I have only addressed, incidentally, the first stages of what happens to mentally disturbed people, who are, of course, in the minority. A lot of these antisocial misfits, as they are described, are too often seriously mentally ill through social and economic reasons.

LL: If they were diagnosed by better qualified doctors – well, what would you do with them?

PT: A police doctor would not be qualified to diagnose. What I am saying is that he could be sufficiently trained, from a lay position, because it could not be anything more than from a lay position, to look for signals that this young man or young woman before him was suffering from some form of mental disorder or distress. Then he would have to call in somebody—

LL: Accepted. But what do you do with them? Do you want better treatment from better qualified staff?

PT: Well, most of them are not receiving any treatment. If one could wave a magic wand, I would train all police doctors and receiving officers, i.e. all medical officers. I would have them trained for six months in being able to detect the signals which indicate mental ill health.

LL: But supposing you had done the things you did when you were 17, would it have been best to send you to Broadmoor, or somewhere else?

PT: But that was the end of the story – there were a lot of stages before that.

LL: Well, all right. But how do you see it?

PT: Graham Young, for example, was sent to Broadmoor at the age of 14, having disposed of all the members of his family.

LL: Was that the right thing to do – at the age of 14?

PT: There was another case, in Rampton, where a young man was put in prison for stealing 11$\frac{3}{4}$d from his mother. He spent 25 years in Rampton.

LL: But they must have thought he was mental.

PT: Then he wrote to Dr McGrath, the Chief Superintendent at Broadmoor, asking to be transferred from Rampton, and within two years Dr McGrath discharged him and he is now working successfully in the building industry. The general consensus of the staff at Broadmoor was that he was not ill at all. This was a case of prejudice.

LL: Well, of course, we know mistakes are made.

PT: Yes, I know. This was a case of prejudice – we are going back to the old days when families could have members put away. He was at Broadmoor when I was there – he went to Rampton at the age of 11. I would imagine that comes under young offender. But his crime was stealing $11\frac{3}{4}$d, and he spent 25 years at Rampton and two at Broadmoor.

LL: Did he seem a mental case when you knew him?

PT: He was the most rational man I have ever come across – happy, cheerful, stable. Perhaps he does not qualify as a young offender.

LL: Let's take Graham Young. He became a serial poisoner. Was it right to send him to Broadmoor?

PT: Yes, but he was discharged at the age of 23 or 24 and went on to kill other people, in the same way as he had killed some of his family.

LL: That was a great mistake—

PT: They have made a lot of mistakes. But that's not your book—

LL: No, but it is interesting.

PT: And out of the Graham Young case in 1974 came the Butler Inquiry and the Sir Carl Aarvold investigations. Reginald Maudling, when he was Home Secretary, instigated them.

LL: Is Young still alive?

PT: He died last year in Parkhurst, at the age of 44.

LL: There is a young mentally disordered offender, if you like. He was sent to the right place.

PT: Those two cases are not relevant to your book—

LL: Oh, but they are relevant. It shows the difficulty. One wants to bring out the nature of the problem. Young is a famous case.

PT: And there are children in Broadmoor, of course, who have committed serious offences. There is a girl of 11 at Broadmoor. I think you ought to go to Broadmoor.

LL: Even so, you would start by providing better arrangements at the early stage?

PT: At the police stage, then at the prison remand stage.

LL: You would try to get better-trained medical officers?

PT: Trained enough to see that there might be a mental history.

LL: That's important.

PT: But then, of course, there is the other side of the fence, that in the high-profile cases there is this prejudice. Not everyone who is arrested sees a police doctor – that is not common practice. I was put in a police cell at eleven o'clock at night. I had a bump on my head and that was the reason I saw a doctor.

LL: But you were already under psychiatric care, weren't you?

PT: Yes, but I was not asked at the police station whether I had a psychiatric history.

LL: You could have used that, couldn't you?

PT: It was used in court, of course, but I had to spend six months in prison in between.

LL: Six months?

PT: In Brixton. I was not asked at the police stage whether I had a psychiatric history, nor was I asked that in prison. It was only when I replied that I was depressed that I was admitted to the prison hospital.

LL: People ask whether prison can improve anyone's character. How can it, when inmates are in the hands of a lot of untrained people?

PT: There are so few beds in special hospitals. Prisons are full of young offenders of which a noticeable number are mentally ill, receiving no treatment.

LL: Would you say that a number of young offenders now in prison or in young offender institutions ought to be hospital?

PT: Yes, a hospital of some kind – not an open hospital, but you can be in special wards. You have got to say that, for humanitarian reasons. And you have to bear in mind that they are going to be discharged when their sentence is completed. What you are discharging, if you have a mentally ill young person in prison, is a

95

time bomb. The person has become a time bomb who is likely to commit a much more serious offence.

LL: You mean because he has been in prison?

PT: And not treated. Being ill in a prison setting, and receiving no treatment in a prison setting, leads to the discharge of someone who is much more likely to commit a serious offence. Prisons, in terms of the mentally ill, are the breeding grounds of recidivists, which is not the purpose of prisons. The mentally ill cannot cope with the prison regime.

LL: Well, to come back to the point I have raised again and again, where would you send them? There are places like St Charles, the youth treatment centre, where there is a staff of 90 and 30 disturbed people. Or Aycliffe. Do you think these people ought to be in hospitals or in some other kind of place?

PT: When you talk about hospitals, here I will agree with you. There is definitely a need for medical institutions to reduce the prison population. There is a need for, say, about seven institutions. The Home Office say that the proportion of the mentally ill in the prison population is equivalent to the number of mentally ill in society. That means that there are approximately in excess of 5,000 people, out of a prison population of about 50,000, who are mentally ill. The trouble is, the Home Office only recognize 300.

LL: There may be 5,000 people who need psychiatric help, but it doesn't mean that all of them ought to be transferred to hospital. People don't all want to go to hospital; they don't like being called nutters.

PT: You have to bear in mind that the purpose of prison is rehabilitation. If the only means of successful rehabilitation is to put them in medical institutions which don't exist in the main, then by leaving them in prison you will eventually discharge a time bomb, somebody who is unstable. The prison system has failed so far as the mentally ill are concerned. Nobody who is mentally ill should ever be sent to prison – they need a secure environment.

I am closing this interview with a case history from the Matthew Trust's files. It speaks more eloquently than I ever could about the plight of the mentally disordered young offender in the British penal system today.

Raffle Moore became an offender at the age of 11. He got in with the wrong set and stole a dinghy – the start of his criminal career.

He became involved in other petty offences and received small sentences.

His mother referred him to the Matthew Trust in 1985. At the age of 17 he was in Chelmsford Prison, so Peter Thompson went to see Raffle one Sunday afternoon. On meeting Mrs Moore later, Peter told her that her son was suicidal and should not be in a cell on his own, locked up for 23 hours a day.

On returning to London, Peter Thompson telephoned Chelmsford Prison requesting that Raffle should be seen by a doctor. He was informed that no medical staff was available over the weekend period. He told them that, in his opinion, Raffle was suicidal and needed to be transferred to the prison hospital for observation. The officer to whom he spoke took notes and said he would look into the matter. By noon the following day, Peter Thompson ascertained that no action had been taken. Raffle had not made any attempt on his life meanwhile. Peter made contact with the Senior Medical Officer and insisted that Raffle should be in hospital. By four o'clock that afternoon, still no action had been taken.

Peter then rang the Letters Editor of the *Guardian* who suggested that he should write to them on the matter. His letter was published the following day (Tuesday). The Governor of Chelmsford, on reading the letter, had Raffle transferred to the prison hospital.

This demonstrates the inadequacies of the system in terms of action by staff at a prison where a psychiatric case is involved. Raffle had bone cancer in the left thigh, was suffering from schizophrenia and moreover was an epileptic. *Yet he had been passed as healthy by the Prison Medical Service.*

Later, as an outcome of the letter in the *Guardian*, Peter was invited by the Home Office to discuss the matter, which resulted in Raffle being transferred to Feltham, where he was given drug therapy. Six months later they notified Peter that they proposed to place Raffle, who was serving a two-year sentence, on parole. Peter, however, requested them to send him to a psychiatric hospital, which they did.

The Matthew Trust has continued to support Raffle Moore to the present day. He has overcome his psychiatric problems and has taken a course in counselling. He is a committed Christian and is looking forward to helping young people with antisocial tendencies which, from his own experience, he is now well qualified to do.

Robert Allen

The National Association for the Care and Resettlement of Offenders

Robert Allen is head of the youth crime section at NACRO and is one of their leading experts on young offenders. At various times I have studied a number of NACRO documents dealing with young offenders for which I believe Robert Allen had a large share of the responsibility. I have had the opportunity of interviewing him more than once. In what follows, I have not tried to distinguish between his views and those of NACRO.

I will begin by quoting two passages from the NACRO Young Offenders' Committee policy paper of December 1991. It is called *Reducing the Use of Custody for Young Offenders.*

1. It has long been accepted that young offenders should be dealt with differently from adults and that youthfulness should be taken fully into account when deciding what response to make. This distinction has most clearly been drawn in respect of juvenile offenders. Since 1908 they have been dealt with in a separate court which has considered their welfare in reaching sentencing decisions. Young adults have also been treated differently in some respects with legal restrictions governing the making of custodial sentences and separate arrangements from adults for those made subject to them.

2. The disadvantages of custodial sentencing for young offenders were highlighted in the Green Paper *Punishment, Custody and the Community* published by the Home Office in 1988. The Paper stated that:
    Most young offenders grow out of crime as they become more mature and responsible. They need encouragement and help to become law-abiding. Even a short period of custody is quite likely to confirm them as criminals, particularly as they acquire the criminal skills from more sophisticated offenders. They see themselves labelled as criminals and behave accordingly.

98

The task therefore has been for all the organizations concerned with youth crime and young offenders to co-ordinate their efforts to ensure that a range of effective and relevant community-based options is available, so that custody is only used in cases where there is genuinely no alternative.

Penal reformers will not find it difficult to accept the arguments quoted, if only because they demand a reduction in the use of custody for offenders of all ages. However, the arguments that young offenders should be treated differently from adult offenders seem to boil down to these:

1. We do not blame young offenders, particularly juveniles, as much as we blame adults who commit the same crimes. Consequently public opinion favours more lenient treatment.

2. Custody is thought to damage young offenders at a malleable stage of their lives more than their seniors. It is more likely to turn them into lifelong criminals. In the case of their seniors, the damage may have become irreversible.

3. To quote the NACRO paper again:
    Perhaps most significant, however, has been the recognition of the limitations and disadvantages of a custodial response in terms of reform or rehabilitation, particularly where the young are concerned. At the same time there has been a recognition of the advantages of dealing with young offenders in the community wherever possible.

Be the theory what it may, I turn to some of the figures. On 30 June 1990, there were 9,155 young offenders in Prison Service establishments (8,917 males and 238 females). There were only 370 juveniles in these establishments, and 8,785 young adults. At first sight, therefore, custody is not used excessively for juvenile offenders. In 1989, however, 2,176 juvenile offenders were sent to Prison Service establishments. This was a dramatic reduction from 1981, when the figure was 7,987. One is bound to welcome this change without reservation. In fact, for 1990 the figure came down to 1,450, a fall of 32 per cent from 1989, and a sharp decrease from 1981. The decline in the number of young adults sentenced to custody was not quite so dramatic, but substantial. In 1985, 26,600 were sentenced to custody; in 1989 the figure was 16,800.

The NACRO document seems to conclude that under the working of the 1991 Criminal Justice Act, there would be a further reduction in the number of young offenders sentenced to custody:

The Act makes a number of provisions focused particularly on young offenders. These include the abolition of custody for 14-year-olds and the redesignation of the Juvenile Court as the Youth Court, which will also incorporate jurisdiction over 17-year-olds. A number of juvenile and adult sentences will be equally available for 16 and 17-year-olds who are considered as 'near adults', such as supervision and probation orders, community service orders, combination orders (probation and community service) and curfew orders.

It seems to be an open question whether some 17-year-olds under the new arrangements would be sentenced to custody who would not previously have been sentenced to it.

In February 1991, Robert Allen published a long and important article in the *Howard Journal. Out of Jail: the Reduction in the Use of Penal Custody for Male Juveniles 1981–1988* begins by calling attention to the marked fall during the 1980s in the number of juveniles sentenced to custody. It was a surprising feature of the Thatcher years: 'The government in power during the entire period of the decline has been an unlikely one to preside over a process of decarceration, although there has been a marked ambivalence in their policy towards juvenile and young adult offenders. The Conservative Party had, prior to 1979, expressed strong views on law and order and the decline of moral standards, which found rapid translation into measures such as the "short, sharp shock".

Robert Allen points out that demographic factors such as the decline in the young population played their part. He states that 'the major reason for the reduction in the numbers sentenced has been an increase of police cautioning'.

The big surprise, however, has turned out to be the effect of the 1982 Criminal Justice Act, which came into force on 24 May 1983. 'It is easy to forget the concern with which academics, penal reform groups and practitioners within the social service departments and Probation Service greeted the proposed legislation.' In the event, the bad features of the Act and the short, sharp shock treatment have proved unworkable. The good features such as the new criteria for sentencing juveniles have proved highly effective.

Social workers of all kinds have played a most beneficial part in bringing about this reduction. Allen gives full credit to the government for what he calls 'a major initiative designed to increase the availability of intensive, intermediate treatment schemes. ... The growth of juvenile justice teams within social services departments or across agencies, and the major reorganizations in many areas, which have followed the IT initiative, suggest that the achievements of the decade have to some extent become enshrined in structures. ... The effective reduction of custody for juveniles in many parts of the country has been due in no small part to the energy, enthusiasm and the commitment of practitioners and managers "on the ground" – the "alternatives to custody" movement has developed an almost crusading zeal.'

100

I break off to quote something that Allen said in a speech delivered on 10 January 1992:

What is interesting from our point of view is that the strategies which are being proposed to reduce the use of custody for less serious offenders, at least, is partly based on the success of approaches to the juvenile justice system over the last ten years. The criteria for custodial sentences, introduced for young offenders in 1982 and strengthened in 1988, are now being extended to offenders of all ages appearing before the courts. Other aspects of criminal justice policy look to borrow from the young offender field; the catch-phrases 'minimum intervention' and 'inter-agency co-operation' are now heard to echo throughout the system and not just in that part of it which deals with young people. Whether the strategy works in respect of all offenders remains to be seen.

To return to young offenders. Various NACRO documents consider the possibility of further reductions in sentencing to custody. NACRO's clearest recommendation to date is this: the government should raise the minimum age at which a young person should be sentenced to detention from 15 to 16 years. In fact one of the NACRO documents wishes the possibility to be explored of ending the detention in a young offender institution of offenders under 18 years of age. If this came about, 15-year-olds, 16-year-olds and 17-year-olds would all be excluded from these institutions.

The question would remain: What would be done with these young people? The word 'custody' is confusing here because in fact a considerable proportion of these young offenders would presumably be transferred to a secure local authority unit. In a general sense I suppose Robert Allen would say that this should occur as seldom as possible. In the last resort he would, I believe, consider that this would be a more constructive arrangement. We are both aware that new resources would be required, not perhaps on a very large scale, to make this possible.

Robert Allen is possessed of a crusading zeal in favour of reducing the number of young people in custody. He insists, however, that a policy of minimal intervention does not mean one of benign indifference. He is well aware that large numbers of young people who now get into trouble have fairly unsatisfactory backgrounds and have often been abused at home. He is a dedicated believer and a practical champion of inter-agency collaboration. As I write, I have two important NACRO documents in front of me on the prevention of youth crime. I will quote the main headings of their recommendations:

1. An inter-agency strategy for reducing youth crime.

2. The role of school and education support services.

3. The contribution of youth, community and leisure services.

4. Wider support for children, young people and families.

NACRO urge the government to provide financial support for families and young people as part of an overall policy to limit crime.

In the first instance we, as other organizations are doing, would ask the government to reinstate income support for young people aged 16 or over who cannot find training or a job; and award young people aged 16 or over who are entitled to income support and are living independently the same amount as is paid to over-25-year-olds.

Robert Allen was seconded to the Home Office after I interviewed him – a tribute to the importance of NACRO's work in this area.

Alan Eastwood

Chairman of the Police Federation

Alan Eastwood joined the Metropolitan Police in 1965 – he served as a uniformed officer in East London – and has been National Chairman of the Police Federation since 1985. He is a man of exceptional prudence and at the same time highly articulate.

In April 1992, a few months before I interviewed Mr Eastwood, his Vice-Chairman Mr Richard Coyles delivered a strongly worded address to a Police Federation meeting in Nottingham. Referring to a particular housing estate in Nottingham, he recalled that it had recently been the subject of a major feature in the London *Evening Standard*. The feature claimed that a gang of youths had stormed and terrorized an old people's home – and that the six juveniles involved had a total of 215 previous arrests between them. Mr Coyles told the meeting that these hardened young offenders, some still at school, knew that the courts could do nothing to detain them. 'When the history of crime in Britain in the twentieth century and especially in the 1990s comes to be written,' Mr Coyles declared, 'please God let there be a chapter pointing out the role of legal aid and criminal rights committees of every ilk in boosting the crime figures to over 5 million a year.'

With 1992's general election pending, Mr Coyles had this to say about the manifestos of the political parties: 'In our policing agenda which we have issued to the candidates in this election we have again drawn attention to the problems of juvenile crime *and to the almost total absence of secure accommodation* [my italics].'

Mr Coyles made a very direct point: that the criminal has lost all fear of retribution because we have made punishment a dirty word. Although neither he nor Alan Eastwood might put things in quite

103

that way, the demand for more secure accommodation is, I am quite sure, universal throughout the police.

LORD LONGFORD: Tell me about the attitude of the police towards young offenders.

ALAN EASTWOOD: We welcome cautioning of young offenders, but we are concerned about the youth who is cautioned time and time again. It may be helpful to have one, two or even three cautions, but there seems to be a need to go before someone. That could be a Chief Inspector, Inspector, Chief Superintendent. The child, who has to admit the offence, and their parent or guardians will go before the officer, who will say in effect that this is a very serious thing, you are not going to court but should you reoffend you will go to court.

LL: Would you caution for joy-riding?

AE: It has happened, which has led to the problem where young offenders lose respect for the law.

LL: Cautioning policy was a police initiative and has grown from there.

AE: Yes, being encouraged by government because it keeps people out of the court and the treadmill of the penal system.

LL: Why doesn't the police officer take them to court after several cautions?

AE: If they continue to offend they can be sent to homes which are run by local authorities, which should be secure but are not. The young person goes there, absents himself and reoffends. What can the court do in these circumstances but send them back to the same home?

LL: Where do you send them if you do not send them to custody?

AE: I agree that they should not be sent to official custody, but secure accommodation run by a local authority surely has to be secure. There are some young people who are a danger to society and should be locked up.

LL: As an alternative to official custody it seems clear that there should be more local authority custody, but are you satisfied that local authorities are the best people to provide it?

AE: If they are proper homes, yes. There are no secure places available in the whole of Wales. In a home in Gwent, highlighted by us in a report to government, they were putting serious offenders in a home for orphan children – that is outrageous. These orphan children were being brought up alongside criminals. There has to be proper secure accommodation. The government are aware of this problem.

LL: The local authorities may not do anything about it.

AE: The money should come from central funds or be specially earmarked for this purpose. Unless we do something we will have these young offenders contemptuous of the law because it does not help them, and we should be helping them. We should be helping them at that age or they will go on to a life of crime.

LL: Taking young people, would you say that the police have favoured greater leniency towards under-21-year-olds?

AE: Generally speaking we would have to say that we have not. We are too lenient; we have moved away from rehabilitating offenders to forgiving them, forgetting the most important person who is the victim. We honestly believe that the Youth Courts have lost their power and they must be given back some powers to deal with the youth who constantly offends and is a danger to himself and to society. But he or she should not be sent to prison or places like that, there must be secure accommodation run by local authorities with properly trained personnel, social workers, probation officers and so on. It is a very difficult job and the training must be first class. There has to be a place where society can be confident that these people will be kept out of harm's way until they are rehabilitated.

LL: So there is a feeling that the move to treat young offenders more leniently in the last ten years has been carried too far?

AE: Yes, that would be a very fair assessment.

LL: If the Prime Minister or Home Secretary asked you what to do about young offenders, what would you say?

AE: There has to be proper secure accommodation. This is a crucial point so that the Youth Courts can sentence persistent young offenders who in their view need to be put in these places. Youth Courts should be given back some powers to show the young offender that it is wrong to go to court at that age. It is a joke to many of them – there is no fear of going to court any more. Fear is a word which has been struck from their dictionary almost. It is very important that they have a fear that if they commit crime they will end up in court, and then secure accommodation. We do not want anyone to offend, but certain sections of the youth of today show contempt for all kinds of authority, be they schoolteacher or police officer.

LL: More community policing – is this possible now?

AE: There is no doubt that the presence of uniform on the streets does bring confidence to the public, especially to elderly people who can be frightened by a group of young people. The sight of a uniform is a great reassurance to them. But the problem goes further back than that. If an officer arrests someone, there must be an effective deterrent – an effective court system – at the end of the line. There is none at the moment.

LL: Community service – what do you think?

AE: Good, if you actually do it, and probation orders are a good thing. The problem is that they are insufficiently staffed. Very good in some areas and poor in others. The quality of staff is something everyone complains about, but there is insufficient money for them to do the job. I think everyone in the penal system gives value for money, but there is a need for more.

LL: Is the Federation pressing for more staff?

AE: Yes. The Metropolitan Police have an establishment of 28,000 and the Commissioner needs 6,000 more officers. Too expensive, we are told. We believe that the new inquiry Kenneth Clarke has initiated is looking at police pay. The Royal Commission we requested has been denied us.

LL: A lot of people think the police are well paid.

AE: Yes, but it was the Edmund-Davis report into police pay which resulted in the level of pay we now enjoy. We are not underpaid nor overpaid, but properly paid. We are understaffed, not just in London but all over the country. It is very difficult to give the public the kind of policing they demand. To call for a policeman on the beat is very nice, but you will never get a policeman for every street.

LL: Regarding court procedures, and the right of silence in particular – would you like this to be modified?

AE: We have asked the present Royal Commission that the right of silence should be changed to give us – and the judge – the right to express that fact to the jury in court. There used to be an Act of Parliament, now repealed, for carrying an offensive weapon, where the onus was on the individual to prove that he had this weapon for a lawful purpose. The onus must be in many cases upon the individual to prove. Unfortunately we have this adversarial system where the prosecution has to prove everything, instead of a search for the truth. How can we change the system to be more of a search for the truth so that miscarriages, either way, do not occur? It is a miscarriage of justice if guilty men go free, though not in the same way as innocent men going to prison. The decision to prosecute is taken by the Crown Prosecution Service, but people still blame the police.

LL: Is the CPS better than the old system?

AE: Yes it is better, it is working far better than we expected.

LL: Are there any other points you wish to bring out?

AE: The whole issue hinges on the things I've mentioned. Government must improve on the amount of secure accommodation available to local authorities and it must be purely secure accommodation. Courts must be given back some powers to really deal with young offenders.

LL: If there is secure accommodation, the court can send offenders there.

AE: Yes, but the government seems to want to keep people out of prison. There are still too many young people in prison, and perhaps there should now be a working party to look at offences which carry a term of imprisonment but perhaps should not. In our view prison should be for the person that cannot be allowed outside, the hardened criminal and violent individual. Teachers and schools should really concentrate on the curbing of violence. Bullying begins in the schools.

David Evans

General Secretary of the Prison Officers' Association

David Evans is a former prison officer, and before that he came close to being a junior Welsh International at rugby (a scrum half). He became Assistant Secretary to the Prison Officers' Association in 1970 and its General Secretary in 1979.

LORD LONGFORD: What developments have occurred since the publication of the Woolf Report?

DAVID EVANS: The report has been largely ignored by the government and doesn't appear in any way to be on their list of priorities. We believe that if it costs money to change the Prison Service, this government will ignore Woolf's special pleading. The other problem is that government opinions change with every Home Secretary – and there have been three Home Secretaries in two years. Mr Waddington left after the Strangeways riot; Kenneth Baker's final act before leaving as a result of the 1992 general election was to create the Prison Service Agency, and then Kenneth Clarke begins to announce widespread market-testing under privatization. So ministers are changing policies, and the civil servants don't know the speed or direction of the policies they're meant to follow.

LL: Do you feel no encouragement from the implementation of the 1991 Criminal Justice Act?

DE: Not really, because it was merely a vehicle for the government to contract out much of the work of the Prison Service, and the vehicle for market-testing the Prison Service which will have to compete for its own work. Nothing positive – only a means to an end.

108

LL: Some people have managed to extract more encouragement from it. Are they rather too hopeful?

DE: There is no sign of a positive agenda for the Prison Service as it affects prisoners, which is what really matters. That's what determines riots, disturbances, attacks upon inmates by inmates. None of these issues was addressed in the Criminal Justice Act and consequently it will have a negative influence.

LL: Do you expect to see more people going to prison?

DE: I think it's inevitable.

LL: The Home Office forecasts even predict it.

DE: By the turn of the century we will have five or six thousand more prisoners in the service. If that's the consequence of the new Criminal Justice Act, I don't see any positive influences in that legislation.

LL: When I met Father Gerald Ennis, for 14 years a prison chaplain, three of them at Feltham, I asked him why conditions had fallen recently. He attributed it to Fresh Start, which had reduced the service cover available.

DE: I think that's true. Fresh Start has many creditable aspects, but locally it has denied institutions the staff to provide proper levels of supervision and security. This means in practical terms that young offenders are locked up for longer and therefore enjoy few, if any, out-of-cell activities. They will bully more and it contributes significantly to the number of offenders committing suicide or self-abuse.

LL: The Governor of Feltham says that he needs another 40 staff. Would you agree?

DE: I don't know the precise level, but I have every faith in the fact that more staff are essential if staff and the Governor are to provide a regime which can prevent people committing suicide.

LL: More staff is one solution, but if you were a dictator what else would you do?

DE: Some policies – particularly economic – have serious social consequences because, for a start, young people are not going to work. This has an obvious effect on people's behaviour, a very negative effect if people can't ever imagine what it would be like to work. The government must address that very seriously.

LL: This is particularly relevant to young offenders, but not only to young offenders.

DE: If you offer no hope, it's inevitable that people will rebel and feel that they don't share society's values. The government has to live up to its responsibility not to perpetuate a permanent criminal class going in and out of the prison system.

LL: There has to be a drive to reduce the numbers of young people in prison – but what's the alternative? One answer is to send them to local authority secure units, but unlike social workers, prison officers aren't qualified to look after these people.

DE: If government denies local authorities the necessary finance to provide care in the community, the local authorities can't and won't tax the individual in order to provide for community care. The vast majority knows this is a cost to be borne by all of society, and government should provide the finance. In the circumstances, it's inevitable that young people end up on the streets or incarcerated in prison.

LL: To get back to my question, do you think that prison officers are less well qualified than social workers?

DE: I don't think that's so. Every individual case should be considered on its merits – you can't generalize. Prison officers are highly qualified and they have personal skills they use; they are dealing with bad behaviour and are used to it.

LL: Should they have longer training?

DE: That is essential.

LL: Prison nursing officers get six months of specialized training. Should all officers get six months of training?

DE: Initial training time should be 24 months, partly institutional, partly in other services. It should involve learning from psychiatrists, probation officers, police officers, then back to training school for reinforcement in personal skills. Criminological and personal qualifications should be recognized – to encourage promotion. Then we can get a better Prison Service.

LL: Some people have suggested more training in therapy. Would that help?

DE: It wouldn't make a significant difference. Of course there are clinical areas where you have to be highly trained, but we are talking here about care and simple humanity.

LL: At one time there was concern that prison officers might become social workers!

DE: Prison and probation officers should form a single service. I have always held this view. We're dealing with criminals at different stages of their career, and I see no reason why there shouldn't be an interchange of staff within a united service. This would be beneficial to existing services and improve still further the quality of care.

LL: That's an ideal. How far would the Prison Officers' Association agree?

DE: This is my personal view. I think that the Prison and Probation Services could offer good ideas to each other. We must consider the quality of service we're providing.

LL: The Probation Service hate the word 'punishment'.

DE: The vast majority of prison officers have an excellent relationship with their prisoners – they have to, otherwise there would be fights on landings every day. They have to get together on a daily basis, and in the main they do. The greatest skill a prison office can have is to say 'no' agreeably to a prisoner.

LL: So the longer the training the better?

DE: Certainly.

Harry Fletcher

*Assistant General Secretary of the National
Association of Probation Officers*

As the Assistant General Secretary of the National Association of
Probation Officers, Harry Fletcher is responsible for campaigning
and for relations with the press and parliament. He was Senior Social
Worker at the National Council for One-Parent Families from 1976
to 1983, where he was responsible for casework and campaigning.

LORD LONGFORD: What are the present aims of the Probation
Service?

HARRY FLETCHER: The traditional aims of the Probation Service are
to advise, assist and befriend. These have now been expanded: to
confront the offender with the effects of the offence, to supervise
him in the community with the object of preventing further offences,
and to help him to reconstruct his life. The Probation Service came
into being in 1912, very much non-conformist in origin, but before
that time those who were already doing this work were known as
court missionaries.

In 1986, John Patten at the Home Office set out to induce the
judiciary to make more sophisticated use of the Probation Service
with regard to youths under the age of 21, and to place more faith
in its possibilities. He felt that probation officers should be pushed
more into social control than into social work. There was much
discussion, followed by a White Paper: *Punishment in the Community*. The probation officers' objections were that the proposed
reforms went too far and would turn them into community prison
officers.

The White Paper was followed by the 1991 Criminal Justice Act,
which sets out three main objectives:

112

1. To create a new sentencing framework whereby custody was to be regarded as a last resort. Speaking of young people, this is a general aim unless the offence is serious, though 'serious' has not been defined.

2. To introduce new non-custodial sentences.

3. To create a Youth Court, replacing the old Juvenile Courts by raising the age limits.

LL: Do you consider that this Act is likely to lead to a reduction in the number of young offenders taken into custody?

HF: We do not yet know how the judges will interpret it. It is something of a shot in the dark. But the hope is that the combination of the new sentencing framework and the less formal atmosphere of the new Youth Court will lead to a more constructive approach generally to young offenders, and an overall reduction in indicted offences. The fear is that the absence of a definition of 'serious' will give rise to a range of interpretations in different parts of the country – more liberal in some parts and harsher in others.

LL: You mentioned other alternatives. What are they?

HF: First of all probation becomes a sentence, instead of an alternative to prison. The judge can say: 'I am not going to sentence you today but will ask the probation officer to prepare a report on your suitability for probation.' If the report is positive, the offender will be put on probation for twelve months. If the offender breaches probation, then he or she will be brought back to court. Every probation order is now turned into a sentence, with one important proviso: the courts can pass combination orders linking probation with a supervised community service order.

LL: Leaving the Act for the moment, if the government came to you and said that the whole question of young offenders needed a fresh look, what would you say?

HF: I am very gloomy about it; I think that crime overall has doubled over the last decade, though there has been a fall where young people are concerned. In 1979, 164,000 were cautioned and found guilty, but by 1989 the number had fallen to 99,000. The main reasons for this were demography, the increased use of formal and informal cautioning, and diversion from the system to community-based alternatives.

There is no simple solution. The evidence would suggest that fewer juveniles are being processed by the criminal justice system and therefore avoiding institutionalization. It may be that informal and formal cautioning does not stem the tide of individual petty crime. The important point is to prevent young people being sucked

113

formally into the system. Once this happens, reoffending becomes much more likely.

Why do juveniles get involved in crime? There is no simple factor, but there are a number of contributory causes: lack of work and constructive activities, parents who have given up, an oppressive environment exacerbated by the police or, in the case of Northern Ireland, by the army and the paramilitaries. Crime, such as joy-riding, offers a challenge to the authorities, the opportunity to show off, the ability to drive fast, to impress your friends and to make money.

Most of this is beyond the capacity of unsupported parents to put right. There are a lot of ideas in the UK, but they tend to be project-based as opposed to nationally-driven programmes. There appears to be a consensus across government departments on youth policy. The emphasis in current thinking is based on crime prevention.

Britain might well learn from France. During the long, hot summer of 1981, there were numerous riots. The French authorities reacted by creating national and local agencies in a co-operative way. In the short term the juveniles were taken out of the conditions that led to the offending and were offered summer and related activities across the board. In the long term, the drive was to change the environment that led to the criminal activities. Inter-agency drives on education, literacy, employment and leisure activities were pro-moted. That is a national, co-ordinated youth policy, which is well resourced, therefore avoiding the demand for instant funding which affects British projects. In the last ten years in France, there has been a fall in crime of about 10 per cent. Over 100,000 young people are involved in these activities.

But to come back to the 1991 Criminal Justice Act: if the offence is very serious or the offending is persistent, then the youth should be placed in an institution where the stay should be as constructive as possible. Feltham is really the antithesis of what an institution of this kind should be. The units are much too big and bullying is rife. I am 100 per cent behind Lord Justice Woolf's insistence on small units and on the importance of young people being kept as near to their families as possible, to allow daily visiting.

LL: How would you set about building small units?

HF: I'd take somewhere like Feltham and subdivide it into seven or eight different prisons. Wormwood Scrubs was intended to be four different prisons, each complete with its own staff, but the whole set-up broke down and no longer works.

LL: If you are going to keep young offenders out of these places, what do you do with them instead?

114

HF: Once these young people are in custody, they are to all intents and purposes finished. The figure is an 80 per cent reoffending rate. The main points for the future are, first, diversion from the criminal justice system – keep them at home with family support. This has to be voluntary, otherwise they are in the system. The youth's family agree, as a condition of not being formally cautioned or formally charged. Second, cautioning: here the aim is to establish national cautioning, based on consistent general principles in which the courts and public may have full confidence. Third, if they have to go into the formal system, hold them at the lowest possible point. Finally, if the youth has to go down, the regime must be as constructive and relevant to the outside world as possible.

LL: This idea of a voluntary scheme, which you are forced by the authorities to join. Do you favour it?

HF: Society will not countenance nothing being done. Take a youth of 14 being charged with shop-lifting. He or she will be seen at the police station by the Inspector and told that, on this occasion, a formal caution is to be given. The parents will be brought in. After three cautions the offender will be brought before magistrates. If at the age of 17 he or she starts to commit burglary, the view is taken that enough is enough. Most of the people working with youth think that we have broadly got it right and manage to turn round a fairly large number of those making up our case-load.

LL: Before they get as far as probation they are cautioned, coupled with a recommendation that they go to some sort of youth club – meaning caution coupled with pressure?

HF: There are a number of innovative projects to divert them from the system at an early stage. In Derbyshire, for example, they have developed a whole range of activities to reduce the need for sending to custody or other residential facilities. Remand fostering is one, whereby young offenders were remanded to foster care, the breakdown of which is reported to be very rare. Support for the placements is provided by juvenile justice workers. According to one report, the situation sometimes improves to the extent that bail may be granted with a support programme. Of the others in Derby, 23 per cent were remanded to family centres, 16 per cent to children's centres with educational facilities and only a very few to lodgings or to prison.

LL: Do you feel that this is an extension of State control or ordinary probation?

HF: We are dealing with such a large group of people – 140,000, before we look at all the people being cautioned. Of that group, most are going to be under 25 so solutions will have to be graded. Keep the petty people out of the system; when the offending starts to be serious, try to break the spell by using a probation centre. Of those currently in probation centres and hostels, more than half have already been to prison. So long as probation centres and hostels remain cheaper than custody they are all right, but as soon as the costs start to equate there is no longer an argument. It would be interesting to know the average weekly cost of holding somebody in Feltham compared with an ordinary probation centre.

LL: What about serious offenders? If you take serious offenders under 18, are they to be kept out of prison custody and, if so, should they be in secure units or not?

HF: There are not many of them. Those young offenders who have committed serious offences are going to be sent to secure units. We are talking of fewer than a hundred at any one time, but they are convicted of very serious crimes like murder and sexual assault.

LL: The people I met on the Nightingale Wing at Feltham must have committed some quite serious crimes. They were having a marvellous time. Do you not think that people like that should be a local authority secure unit?

HF: I have doubts about local authority social work departments; there is role conflict involved. I think transferring offenders to local authorities would raise questions as to their perceived role. I am not bothered as to whether the Prison Department or the Department of Health is in charge, it is what they provide that is important. If the young offender is to be incarcerated, it must be in a way which will help him or her to be rehabilitated. They should receive relevant training for when they come out. Keep the Nightingale unit – it could be the model. They have produced a documentary about their work with families. It is an idealistic set-up. The Governor, Joe Whitty, is the best type of man to take this thing forward. 'The more you punish people, the less successful you are' should be the maxim of the criminal justice system.

Stephen Shaw

Director of the Prison Reform Trust

Stephen Shaw, now 39 years old, trained as an economic historian, his doctorate being a study of the Trades Union Congress and its attitude to unemployment between the First and Second World Wars. After a spell of teaching in technical colleges, he became a research officer at NACRO (National Association for the Care and Resettlement of Offenders), followed by a year at the Home Office. He is now the Director of the Prison Reform trust.

LORD LONGFORD: Before we come to young offenders, how do you think that things have changed in the penal reform world over the past few years?

STEPHEN SHAW: A colleague has a rather interesting metaphor for trying to judge the success or otherwise of anything we do. He alleges that, during the First World War, the *Luftwaffe* were able to claim a 'kill' if they had taken part in any sortie in which a British plane was downed. In contrast, the RAF could only claim a 'kill' if they had fired the final shot which brought down the German plane. In trying to judge the influence of a pressure group, we subscribe to the *Luftwaffe* view. If we have asked for something or have campaigned for a change in policy which actually comes about, we claim that as a 'kill' even though other penal reformers have been asking for the same thing.

LL: Well, I am on your side. But on the whole would you say that it has been a successful period?

SS: Over the last ten years, I think that there have been substantial advances in terms of prisoners' rights, which have come about largely

117

as a result of the Strangeways riot in 1990 and the Woolf Report.

LL: So there has been progress since Strangeways?

ss: Yes, indeed, in terms of prisoners' rights. I identify a number of those: the virtual abolition of censorship of mail; the introduction of card phones; some improvements in visiting entitlements; changes in the prison disciplinary system, notably the abolition of what are called Board of Visitor adjudications; the commitment to having a prison ombudsman; the commitment to a code of standards for the prison system, and so on. What has improved hardly at all is the regime of available activities in prisons – access to education, access to work or vocational training. I think, too, that it is questionable whether relationships between prisoners and the prison staff have actually improved. Even so, it is a significant list – mainly as a result of Strangeways and the Woolf Report.

LL: Terrible thing to think that violence pays.

ss: I think that the 1991 Criminal Justice Act—

LL: Ah, now, what is your general view of the Act?

ss: There are many aspects of the 1991 Act that I welcome. As to the net effect of the Act on the prison population, I share your fear that the consequences will be to increase the number of prisoners. Nevertheless, the sentencing structure introduced in the first five or six sections of the Act is a significant advance. The abolition of parole for the vast majority of prisoners is also desirable.

Taken together, the Criminal Justice Act of '91, the Woolf Report and the Government White Paper on the prisons [*Custody, Care and Justice*] make up a significant advance in prison reform. I would add to that in terms of advances – there is no question that the treatment of juvenile young offenders has seen a marked trend against the use of custody in the 1980s.

Those are the advances. On the failures, I think there are several. The first – simply taking the number of prisoners today as compared with 1980 – is that the prison population has increased. We still top the European prison league in terms of the number of people inside. A second failure is in terms of regimes. Prisoners are far less active and spend longer being locked up in their cells today than they did 20 years ago. And I suppose that the most worrying aspect of the whole law-and-order scene, during the 1980s and continuing, is the disproportionate use of prison against black people. I think young blacks are more likely to be stopped by the police, and if they are stopped, are more likely to be searched; if searched, they are more likely to be arrested; and if arrested, are more likely to be charged.

118

If charged, they are more likely to be remanded in custody. If convicted, they are more likely to receive a custodial sentence. I don't think judges are biased. There is a certain amount of research and it is very equivocal in its findings. From my point of view, I think there is bias at each stage. In addition, we know that the prison system recruits disproportionately from the young and disadvantaged. There are a lot of black people living in relatively deprived inner-city areas.

LL: In the field of young offenders, you have mentioned already that there has been this reduction in the use of custody. No doubt, there are a lot of people who deserve some credit – the Thatcher government—

SS: Well, it is a paradox. I am very proud of what has been achieved – the distilled wisdom of research suggests that it is better for young people to be kept out of the clutches of the criminal justice system, out of the clutches of the prison system, and to a very large degree those are the policies which have been followed during the 1980s. It is important to note increased police cautioning for young people, and when young people have actually appeared in court, there has been a strong trend against the use of custody. What is interesting about this is that it hasn't been an isolated trend – it is all the juvenile magistrates across the country operating their own mini-juvenile justice systems, every police force, more or less, individually deciding that this is a better way of tackling youth crime in their own area. On the whole, a remarkable change in attitude of some unlikely people – the police, magistrates and the government.

I doubt we would have predicted this had we said some 15 years ago: 'Do you think all this is likely to happen under a right-wing government?' But I do think that the total failure of the high-profile, short, sharp shock initiative influenced both magistrates' and government thinking. The entertaining aspect of the short, sharp shock policy is that it was the magistrates who did not think it was a worthwhile one to follow.

LL: I thought it was the prison officers who did not like it.

SS: The prison officers did not actually enjoy working in that way – dealing with children of the same age as their own. Bullying children and barking at them did not appeal to them. But the boys liked it, because it was consistent with their own values – it made you terribly fit; the macho element was quite appealing. The paradox was that the boys liked it, but the magistrates did not. And when they did their research they found, of course, that the policy had not made the slightest difference. That was the last time the government

119

actually initiated a policy to crack down hard on juvenile crime. It was a failure – well, it was more than a failure, it was a fiasco. But that fiasco did clear the way for a very different approach.

LL: Do you feel that the amount of service rendered by prison staff has been much reduced since the introduction of Fresh Start?

SS: There is no question that Fresh Start has meant a very significant reduction in the number of staff on duty at any one time. This is particularly true at weekends when, as a consequence of Fresh Start, in many prisons there are only half as many staff on duty as there would be during the week. This has had a very damaging impact on regimes. This is why, at Feltham, for instance, the boys are locked up virtually all day on Saturday and Sunday.

LL: During the week, too. It is incredible.

SS: I would be cautious in assuming that reduced staffing levels necessarily mean more restrictive regimes. The Prison Officers' Association will always say that you cannot guarantee decent conditions for prisoners unless you increase staffing levels. I think it is true, of course, at Feltham. But I would be much more cautious in assuming that that applies everywhere. I am on record as saying that the only way of coping at Feltham is either by reducing the number of prisoners or by increasing the number of staff. I have no doubt about that. But I do not assume that that is the case in every prison. There are some prisons where staffing levels are more favourable and it would be possible to deploy staff in such a way as to allow prisoners out of their cells more frequently.

May I say something else about Feltham and institutions for young people generally? We now have a system for dealing with young offenders not so very different from that for women. There are relatively few institutions, particularly for juveniles, and at the moment the prison estate is made up of relatively large institutions. As a consequence of this, in the case of women, they may be hundreds of miles from their homes. In Holloway, for example, the women come from an area that extends from the Wash to Bristol. Feltham has a catchment area for juveniles not very different – boys come from Cornwall, after all. I would like to get away from the idea of large institutions both for women and for juveniles. I would like to see a larger number of much smaller places, call them hostels, residential centres or whatever.

LL: Feltham has about 800 people. Are you thinking of places for a hundred people?

SS: That sort of size or even smaller, a larger number of small institutions. Feltham must be the largest concentration of young delinquents in the whole of Europe.

LL: Supposing the Home Secretary were to ask you how to go about changing the system. How would you respond? Would it mean building a lot of new places?

ss: It might mean closing a place like Feltham, or converting it to some other use. It means, if you like, having mini-prisons or hostels—

LL: But you would have to build these places, wouldn't you?

ss: You would have to spend money either building or converting. This is clearly a long-term policy. After all, they have spent all the money on Feltham within the last ten years. Feltham is a new institution; they must have invested in real terms some £50 million or more. They have spent money on large institutions – that applies to women as well – and I don't think that large institutions are desirable.

LL: Would that fit in with the conclusions of the Woolf Report?

ss: It is consistent with the Woolf Report. Woolf talks about the idea of community prisons. One aspect of the community prison is the idea that within the secure perimeter you might have separate units for young offenders, adults, remands, convicted offenders, perhaps even for men and for women.

LL: You could split up Feltham into a lot of little places, but it still does not cover the fact that inmates would be a long way from home.

ss: Not unless you were also converting other prisons elsewhere in the country. One has to be realistic about it. You will always have difficulty with places like Cornwall and North Wales, because they don't generate enough villains to fill even a small institution.

LL: But that is what one should be aiming at?

ss: Yes, either by building new places or converting existing ones into much smaller units which would enable the young people to be closer to home.

LL: Now let us come to the most difficult part of the subject. Supposing you decide not to send the young people now in custody to penal custody – where do you send them? The Howard League, the Prison Reform Trust and NACRO are pressing strongly that nobody under 15 should go into penal custody. When I was at Feltham recently, news came through that three boys of 15 had been convicted of raping a girl of 13. Well, what do you do with them?

ss: The majority of 15-year-olds who end up in custody have not been convicted of crimes of the gravity of the one you describe. Furthermore, if we are interested in trying to divert young people from future offending, there is some pretty good evidence that the sort of scheme run by social services departments and voluntary organizations – under the general heading of intermediate treatment – are much more successful in reducing future offending than sending somebody to prison.

ll: I really don't think the evidence—

ss: Although under the Home Office policy on young offenders the custody regime is supposed to address the causes of the young person getting into trouble, in practice that is carried out at a much more modest level than is the case under an intermediate treatment scheme.

ll: Of all the people now undergoing intermediate treatment, only a very small proportion are young offenders. At Lambeth, for example, they have nine units, but only one is for young offenders. The truth is that IT schemes vary enormously. One of the problems is that if boys are 16, they ought to be getting work, but if they are having intermediate treatment they can't get a job.

ss: I accept that there are a lot of schemes under the one umbrella, all doing different things. However, I remain an enthusiast for intermediate treatment.

ll: But intermediate treatment is not custody.

ss: There are some young people who are a threat to society, or whose offences are so grave that their liberty has to be removed.

ll: But where do you send them? Take Aycliffe – there are about 120 children and 300 staff, two-thirds of whom are professionally qualified. Some of their young people are very disturbed – I spoke to a senior member of staff who had been bitten three times by one of them. In the Albatross unit at Feltham, they have 20 young people and 8 staff.

ss: Quality and number of staff are a reason for thinking that prison is an inappropriate place for young people. It has also to do with the culture of prison and what prison is about, and what a unit run by social services is about. You may remember the case of the boys who were transferred from Leeds Prison to the new jail at Moorlands. They were moved from Leeds, where they should never have been kept. There were suicides there and oppressive treatment. They were moved to Moorlands and they smashed the place up, partly at least because they wanted to be moved back to Leeds which was 'a *real* prison'. They did not want this modern, well-equipped, caring environment. Now, do we really want to confirm their self-identity as full-time adult villains, when they are actually only children? I don't think we do.

LL: But when you talk about caring for young people, whether a social worker is better able to cope with a young thug of 17 than a prison officer is really a doubtful point.

SS: I say these things, I hope, not in a naive spirit. If we stop sending young people to prison and instead have a number of them in secure units, effectively locked up, I don't think this will make a massive difference. Some of them will still be so disturbed that they will cut their own faces, their hands or their arms, swallow batteries, attack members of the staff, and on release will still constitute a danger to society. It just seems to me that Prison Department custody manifestly has failed. This is not to argue that the social services are necessarily going to deliver all that we want, but it must be a better way of dealing with children than prison.

LL: Some people think that the future might lie with the Probation Service. You might have institutions run by the Probation Service, instead of by prison officers or by the social services. Do you think the Probation Services would be better?

SS: I think that this should be a matter for the social services rather than the Probation Service. Probation's great expertise is in dealing with adult offenders, social services' expertise is in working with children, whether in trouble with the law or not. So, on balance, I would like to see Probation Service involvement diminishing, as indeed it has been. Most supervision orders now are in the hands of the social services.

LL: The Probation Service have always been very equivocal about whether they are ready to exercise control.

SS: Yes, the present standards within the Probation Service make it clear that they are in the business of controlling. They are part of the law-and-order system. I have never understood how they could think that they were not in the business of controlling or reducing crime.

LL: I don't see the way at all clearly. Take Aycliffe, or another place I am going to, St Andrew's in Northampton, a private place for disturbed children. Somehow, or other, local authorities are still involved.

ss: They pay for places.

ll: But at Aycliffe – with a high proportion of staff, highly qualified – people come from all over the country. It does not meet your demand for community-based units at all. You would want several of those.

ss: Yes, you would want several smaller ones.

ll: Take the boy I mentioned earlier who bites people—

ss: It is the level of disturbance that you and I find difficult to credit.

ll: But the Home Secretary might say that if you don't know the answer, nobody else will—

ss: Well, I have indicated the broad thrust. I would like to see the degree to which it would be possible to replace these large institutions with smaller ones. Again, building on what I see as the tremendous gains of the last ten years, having abolished Prison Department custody for 14-year-olds, we should now abolish it for 15-year-olds as well. One consequence of that may be a need to invest further in special units under social services or the Aycliffe model, but my own feeling is that the vast majority of 15-year-olds presently going to prison could be better dealt with under existing community provision.

ll: That is very slight control.

ss: Many probation officers would challenge that description.

ll: To see a probation office once a week – you can commit all sorts of crime in the meantime. Presumably you would be ready for more intensive supervision?

ss: That's right. I am not so lily-livered that I think that when somebody breaks into your home or attacks you in the street you just say: 'Oh well, I am sorry about that.' Their behaviour should be challenged. In a sense what you are trying to do is rebuild in the young person a sense of the moral values they so singularly lack.

ll: You have confidence in community service orders?

ss: The research I did some years ago indicated that there was a wide range of community service orders – some better organized than others – but that in general people did turn up to do the work. In a minority of cases, but in a significant minority, they found the

124

work fulfilling in itself. Some of them – I would not want to exaggerate the number – do actually go on from having been on a community service order to do the same work in a voluntary capacity. Somebody described community service as 'the best punishment invented this century'. I think it has an awful lot going for it. It is definitely a punishment, because it deprives you of your time; it also means that some work is done which is of benefit to society at large. It makes constructive demands on the offender. I think it commends itself not only to our trendy penological thinking, but to those who take a rather more robust view.

LL: Would you favour an extension of it?

SS: When you are talking about a young offender, the difficulty is to decide at what age it is proper to insist that he does community work which may involve him in being some distance from his home. So there are problems with very young people. But with adult offenders, the only thing stopping further expansion in community services is our own imagination in thinking up the number of schemes which could be run.

LL: I think your programme will take a long time to bring about.

SS: If you don't dream dreams, you never achieve anything. You know that far better than me.

III
Relevant Individuals

Lord Mancroft of Mancroft

Chairman of the Addiction Recovery Foundation

As a young man – he is now 36 – Lord Mancroft's life was governed by an addiction to heroin, cocaine, alcohol and pills. After many attempts to find a cure in Britain, he finally made a full recovery as a result of the professionalism and expertise of the Hazleden Foundation in the United States who run the well-known Minnesota Method – all of which and more Lord Mancroft had the courage to tell the House of Lords in a debate in January 1991.

LORD LONGFORD: Can you describe what led you into drug-taking – was it gradual?

LORD MANCROFT: I first got involved with drugs when I left school and started with them for the same reason small boys plays football – others were doing it. I was in London because I was going to join the army, had a car accident and could not join after all. I had seven operations over two years and lived in London without work, rather bored, rather disillusioned and so wasted time, killed time, having been on too many over-prescribed painkilling drugs. That's why I started to take them – mainly cannabis, progressing up the ladder.

LL: Is it a natural progression?

LM: It used to be – now it doesn't happen so much. Many get on the ladder higher up; it's more extensive now and some will start on crack or ecstasy or ice without marijuana or cannabis first, though some will start on a drug and remain on the same one. The idea is that all drugs are the same. Marijuana or cocaine are still addictive; one of the most addictive is alcohol. I drank alcoholically since I first took beer at Eton, because I would drink to get drunk.

129

Although it is an established fact, it is not sufficiently realized that alcoholism is a primary disease. If a doctor wrote a piece on the high incidence of measles in a public school, for example, it would be acceptable, but if he wanted to write about the pupils' drinking habits, the very idea would be discredited and brushed under the carpet. The appalling moral aspect is that alcoholism is seen as a nuisance – it is actually a disease.

LL: Surely there is a moral aspect? Surely you give way or overcome it?

LM: No – alcoholism is a disease and recognized as such by the World Health Organization, though not by the British government. You can't recover from alcoholism through moral courage any more than moral courage can help mend a broken leg. It can take a moral decision to stop, but it's a health decision too.

LL: Boredom must have played a large element – alcohol too?

LM: Yes, from an earlier stage. In the absence of other drugs I would use alcohol. I was a poly-addict; you swap and don't mind what you take.

Smoking only rarely has an effect on health. Drugs affect your mental, financial, emotional, career and sexual states and your legal status. Smoking is an addiction but no one sees smokers as moral reprobates. Two glasses of wine do not make a moral reprobate, but two bottles do.

LL: But surely there is alcohol abuse and drug abuse?

LM: Historically, alcohol has often been used to heighten social occasions in many, many societies. There is an interesting dilemma as to why one type of drug, alcohol, is encouraged by society but another, marijuana or cocaine, is outlawed.

Existing legislation is a muddle, ill thought out, illogical and needing urgent review with a fresh mind. I don't think it desirable that all drugs should be available on all street corners, but addicts should not be driven underground to behave like criminals.

LL: If the Prime Minister asked you for a solution, what would it be?

LM: No longer make it criminal for individuals to possess limited quantities of drugs. You must and should make supply, sale and manufacture and importing of drugs a major offence.

LL: There's no logic to that, surely?

LM: Drug-taking is very destructive. As a society, increasing numbers

130

are destroying their lives by using them. By limiting drugs coming in, you limit the damage. If it was made legal tomorrow there would be a bit of an increase, but evidence from all over the world shows there would not be a wholesale increase in the numbers taking drugs.

LL: You would make it no longer illegal even for heroin?

LM: Heroin is not much more dangerous than alcohol. It doesn't make you irrational; the only effect of importance is to slow reactions, so you should not drive or use machinery. It is currently illegal to drive with alcohol. Drugs affect an individual, his family and society. The fact that drugs are illegal and expensive currently causes greater financial problems to the State than the health aspect. If drugs were legal, drug street-crime costs would drop. As a country, drugs cost us about £1.5 billion annually on courts, insurance, police, social services and private individuals' time. That money could be used in dealing with the health problems. There would be no mugging, no break-ins in order to support the habit.

LL: I started the New Horizon Youth Centre for drug addicts. Thirty died in the first year or two.

LM: It should not be encouraged, but more die of alcohol than heroin. Heroin addicts die because they have to be underground and use dirty syringes.

LL: Some were registered.

LM: If it wasn't illegal – and I'm not taking a moral stand – people would not have to hide. Usually addicts don't come forward because of a fear of the law. It would be out in the open and easier to deal with. Another problem is that the police do not enforce the law consistently from area to area. Some let them off with a caution, some send them to court immediately. This is now starting to change and be more consistent.

LL: What about young offenders? Did drugs cause you to turn to crime, for example?

LM: I did break the law, by possessing heroin. Contemporaries I met took to crime to get money for drugs.

LL: Doesn't it lead to violent crime?

LM: The main level of crime is the requirement for money for drugs. Dealers get violent. Legalization would eliminate black-market dealers; at present, paying for the addiction leads to prostitution and pimping. Most street-walkers are addicts. They would come off the streets. There are a variety of good reasons to remove drug-taking

131

from the criminal sphere. About 50 per cent of prisoners are alcoholics or drug-dependent. Drug-taking clogs up courts, prisons, the police, with a huge cost in damage and fear.

LL: You would make drugs legal but restrict the amount?

LM: To the level of personal use. For example, if a man went down the street with a case of whisky, he could not say it was for his personal consumption for a day. However, one bottle would be for his daily use. If a man had ten grains of heroin, it would not be for his use today. You would need to set a ceiling on the amount allowable per day. Anyone with more would automatically be charged with supplying. The drug itself would be obtainable legally from special centres.

LL: I know a drug importer – he would argue it wasn't wrong. The judge said in summing-up that the man had been 'firing a machine gun into a crowd'.

LM: There is an element of truth in that; drugs are very destructive. I see the moral dilemma in the State supplying drugs said to be dangerous. But they already allow it through registered drug-addict schemes. The drug-addict scheme in Liverpool didn't cure the drug problem – it merely cured the crime problem attached to it.

LL: It is difficult to prove that drugs lead to crime any more than alcohol.

LM: There will always be people who commit crime just for kicks, not because they are addicts.

LL: Cases of drunks smashing things up—

LM: Family disputes and drunken husbands, yes. It is always danger-ous to be driving, using machinery with drink or drugs. The crime is using both together – these should remain offences. You can go overboard in privacy. There need to be stricter checks in employ-ment.

LL: Are you involved with any drug rehabilitation schemes at present?

LM: The Addiction Recovery Foundation, Phoenix House, the Drug and Alcohol Foundation, among others.

LL: Would you regard it as a curse? Your negative reform to legalize drugs is only a part of your efforts.

LM: You must not change the law without a major advance in the treatment of those who abuse drink and drugs. There is denial of the problem by the sufferer, and by family and society. Most addicts need crisis and the most obvious crisis is going before the courts. Courts rarely send people to prison for drug-related crime, and even fewer for possession. For example, courts can impose probation with the condition that you attend a treatment programme. Get a good report and you'll have a good chance; a bad one, and I'll throw the book at you. It is possible to help everyone, not only those who want to be helped, but we need much better counselling. Most treatment programmes in Britain are very poor. Some people will need inpatient treatment, some can be outpatients.

Treatment programmes should be provided by the voluntary sector under contract. That's where you find the expertise, but local and national government loathe contracting out. There should be a reallocation of existing funds – they are very badly spent by the statutory agencies, with endless committees and outcome studies. Good treatment works, absolutely conclusively – but some existing programmes are incredibly inefficient.

LL: What about your own treatment?

LM: I went to the Hazleden Foundation in Minnesota in 1982 because there was no equivalent facility in Britain. I paid privately but the cost overall was no more expensive than an equivalent NHS bed. It is a fallacy that private health care is expensive.

LL: St Charles has 100 staff to look after 30 patients and a place there costs the State £100,000 a year.

LM: One staff to one patient is about right. In pure cost terms the private sector is probably cheaper because it doesn't have the NHS's huge overheads and financial incompetence.

My treatment was simple – physical detox lasting two or three days including heroin detox. Then straight into the programme, a twelve-step one devised by Alcoholics Anonymous over 50 years ago. It works. There is aftercare in AA meetings – they're growing in Britain at an enormous rate. I was there about six months in all. There are now about 14 treatment centres in this country in the private and voluntary sectors but they don't have enough patients and several are liable to go bust, though they get enquiries every day. Most of the therapy is provided by trained counsellors, many ex-addicts themselves. In Britain, their training is ignored because their qualifications are not recognized here. They are either unqualified or they have an American qualification. They receive patronizing contempt from NHS doctors.

LL: So if you're an SRN you have to be trained but not if you are a counsellor?

133

LM: The US has higher standards and we need them here. Too many people are untrained and do more harm than good.

LL: Drugs and drink were ruining your life. People's lives are ruined, aren't they?

LM: Yes, by both alcohol and drug abuse. There are recreational drinkers, but there are no recreational heroin users who aren't addicted. There are some recreational cannabis and marijuana users, and a very few of cocaine. It can be difficult to draw the line. Where's the line between one bottle of whisky a day and a few glasses each night? All addicts abuse; not all abusers are addicts.

LL: You say that drugs should be legalized. Most people would say that means more drugs would be taken, more people damaged.

LM: Yes, it would bring direct damage to about 10 per cent of users. But there is no evidence to suggest that overall drug-taking would markedly increase.

LL: So there would be no increase in the recreational use of heroin?

LM: Anyone who is using heroin is going to become an addict anyway. When these things are illegal they are hidden, encouraging health and crime problems.

There is no perfect solution. We don't need more lawyers and sociologists here, but we do need to avoid hysterical screaming. It is much more constructive to debate it gently and really look at it. The one thing that is absolutely clear is that the present system does not work, and it's getting worse.

LL: Baroness Wootton recommended legislation to decriminalize some drugs 20 years ago. The artistic world wanted it; very few other people said they did.

LM: It would make sense to legalize it, simply because of the huge costs of crime and health care. In the long run treatment centres are infinitely cheaper than prison and reoffending.

LL: But surely it is still very costly?

LM: I founded a project in Nottingham about four years ago where the Health Authority paid a clinic for bed space. It cost £400,000 for 25 people for one year – inpatients. You need 6 nurses, 4 therapeutic, 4 admin and 4 ancillary staff. Twenty-five beds is about the most efficient for economies of scale without losing the personal touch. This kind of thing could work if national and local government contracted services out. They have no expertise in treating drink and drugs at all.

LL: You're not advocating privatizing it?

LM: No, not privatizing – use the voluntary sector.

Anthony

I have known Anthony for more than 17 years, and on more than one occasion have given evidence as to character in a court on his behalf. He has been to prison many times for short periods for minor offences like accepting stolen cheques, but never for anything remotely violent. He is intelligent and affectionate, and I once asked him why he persisted in doing these things. 'If I could answer that question, I would not do them,' he replied.

LORD LONGFORD: Can you remember when you first broke the law? Was it a moment of any significance?

ANTHONY: I can't recall my exact first breach of the law, but I was breaking the rules from quite an early age. At about 12 or 13 I was conscious of being in breach of the rules.

LL: But surely that would be true of a large number of your contemporaries?

A: I suspect that it's true to a greater or lesser extent of most kids. I'm not sure that most of them would be aware they were breaking the rules and I think that may be significant. I was aware of it and quite enjoyed it. One of the perverse characteristics of my life is that I have enjoyed crime. Most criminals have a more basic reason. I actually get turned on to an extent by it.

LL: Can you remember at what point you broke the criminal law?

A: From about 15 I was shop-lifting, drinking, stealing and lying.

LL: Were you alone it that? Or were you one of a gang?

136

A: Yes to both questions. At times I acted alone, at others with my peers.

LL: When were you first brought before the courts?

A: 19.

LL: What happened to you in the court?

A: I was placed on probation with residence at a mental hospital.

LL: For how long?

A: Four months, I think.

LL: When you emerged, did you have a different attitude to breaking the law?

A: No. I was considerably more screwed up coming out than going in.

LL: Do you mean that you were more rebellious?

A: No. I began making repeated suicide attempts.

LL: When did you first go to prison?

A: I was 22 and I got three months.

LL: Looking back, would you say that there were steps that could have been taken by the authorities or by your parents that could have prevented you from following this downward course? In other words, if you had a son today who was involved in petty crime and proceeded to prison, would you consider from your experience that there was anything you could do about it?

A: I doubt it. It is just possible that if something had excited me more than crime then it would have taken its place. Strangely, looking back, I think that I might have been converted by taking an active interest in politics, but I would have been a revolutionary and possibly a dangerous one at that.

LL: A lot of young men get their thrills from sport. Did that never appeal to you?

A: No. Until later in life I never really had any interest in sport.

LL: Suppose you had been taken to a child psychiatrist early in life – could that have helped you?

A: I was. And no.

LL: What then is it that causes the problem as you see it?

A: From a very early stage in my life, I began to detach myself from myself and create and live in worlds of my own making – fantasies. I fell in love with fantasy and I still am in love with it. I do not see myself as a fixed entity, but each morning I can choose who I want to be and I have a mental identity and equipment to live that part. That is what turns me on. That is my life. I act for real.

LL: Would you say that you are suffering from a mental illness?

A: As long as I stay within the law, I think I am very eccentric. When I stray outside it, I may or may not be suffering from a mental illness. The doctors cannot agree.

LL: You are on your own showing a singular man. What kind of steps help people like you when they are young?

A: I am in the school of the agnostics. I do think that TLC is a very good approach, but sometimes hard discipline works or appears to work better. I think that time and care and interest are the keys.

LL: Do you think that we send too many young people to penal custody?

A: Yes. We send too many people to penal custody full stop. But for the young the policy should be one of trying to discover what makes them do wrong things and talking to them about it and gaining their trust and trying to counsel them against wrong. Ideally, that should be in the home and with the involvement of their parents and family. I do not like institutions and I don't think that the offending juvenile does either. But what then of the persistent offender? In that case I think that some form of residential care is necessary, but it has to be as homelike as possible. I also think that it is not a good idea to allow kids to know how much these places cost because that simply gives them a badge to wear.

LL: What kind of people could help young offenders in the way you suggest?

A: Multi-disciplinary. But the most important thing is that the helpers actually care for their charges and are interested in them. Some of the helpers therefore need have no qualifications at all except for their humanity.

LL: There are a great many centres of one kind or another, some run by local authorities, some run otherwise, which are non-residential – intermediate treatment centres. Do you favour them?

A: Yes. If in conjunction with the family they settle and manage the

138

individual, they have the advantage of keeping him home-based and being cheaper.

LL: Do you think that more use of psychiatry should be made in dealing with young offenders?

A: No. Psychiatry tends to stigmatize and the last thing you want is to stigmatize further someone who already has problems.

Dr Gordon Burnett

Consultant Psychiatrist, St Andrew's Hospital, Northampton

A little over a year ago I published *Prisoner or Patient*, a study of mentally disordered offenders. Three main points arose from all the evidence. The first was that effective arrangements ought to be made to diagnose convicted persons and in a good many cases they should be sent for some time to hospital rather than to prison. In the second place, the standard of psychiatric care in prison should be vastly improved and the Prison Medical Service should be integrated with the NHS. And finally, care for mentally disordered offenders in the community should be turned into a reality instead of being, as at present, little better than a farce.

For the present book I turned in the first instance to Dr Paul Bowden, a distinguished psychiatrist at the Maudsley Hospital and Brixton Prison. He had given most valuable evidence when I was writing *Prisoner or Patient*. Rather to my disappointment, he took a pessimistic view of the amount of assistance that psychiatrists could render young offenders. He pointed out that schizophrenia, for example, does not usually develop until later in life. He takes, I think, a more limited view than some of his professional colleagues of the possibility of treating personality disorders. He was aware of the claims by reputable hospitals about the progress made by their psychiatric patients, but he said that he was yet to be shown after-care results that impressed him. I told him – as he well knew – that research into the post-treatment lives of those who had attended the St Charles Youth Treatment Centre had appeared to be encouraging. He smiled, and wondered whether the same patient would not have done equally well without the treatment.

Dr Bowden did not, of course, deny that good work was being done, and helpful as always, he pointed me in certain directions. In

140

particular, he mentioned the Young Persons Unit at St Andrew's, Northampton. In what follows I concentrate on my visit there in August 1992.

Dr Gordon Burnett, consultant psychiatrist at St Andrew's, took great trouble to help me understand what was being achieved. Dr Burnett takes a well-justified pride in the Young Persons Unit. 'We have,' he said, 'a national and an international reputation.' This was fully confirmed from other sources. The unit receives referrals from all over the country, the usual referral sources being social services or health authorities. The facility in fact consists of two medium-secure units, the John Clare Unit and the Jeffrey Hawkins Unit, and an open rehabilitation ward. It usually accepts individuals of 14 to 25 years of age.

I asked Dr Burnett what proportion of the young were convicted offenders. 'A recent internal audit indicated that 55 per cent have a previous history of offending,' he replied. He went on, however, to point out that this was not the whole story. All patients who are admitted to the Young Persons Unit are detained under a section of the Mental Health Act (1983) or the Children Act (1989) – only a minority in the latter case. Dr Burnett made the significant comment that 'Although only 55 per cent of our admissions have a history of offending, it is interesting to consider how many would have gone on to reoffend or to offend in the first place if they had not received adequate treatment'.

I asked him about the length of stay in the unit. This depended, he explained, on the needs of a particular individual, but a recent internal audit suggested a mean stay of ten months in the medium-secure unit and a further six months in the open rehabilitation ward. Before coming to St Andrew's, the young people had usually been in care or in some other facility. 'Our audit indicated that 39 per cent of our residents come from another hospital, 27 per cent from other secure units, 16 per cent from another specialist unit such as a specific adolescent assessment unit, 11 per cent from hostels and 5 per cent from remand centres.' He carried me along with him when he insisted: 'In view of the fact that we are currently at 70 per cent occupancy, we clearly have the capacity to provide a greater service to juvenile offenders.'

'Our Hospital Unit,' Dr Burnett explained, 'provides a comprehensive approach to treatment that facilitates the development of the individual in a variety of areas. The general ward programmes are based on behavioural principles.' This means the encouragement of learning skills to replace 'inappropriate behaviour'. Dr Burnett has no illusions about the problems confronting him. 'In order to treat the difficult and challenging individuals who are referred to us

141

we need to be able to contain and manage the disruptive and damaging behaviours that they sometimes display.' He insists, however, that security must not be overdone. 'The appropriate balance must be attained between containment and treatment. Our units are specifically geared towards treatment and so only use the least restrictive measures necessary to manage problem behaviour such as physical aggression.' The phrases may sound abstract, but Dr Burnett is dedicating his life to giving them reality. The focus of the programme is on understanding the reason for the inappropriate behaviour and providing carefully targeted and individualized treatment. For example, in the case of physical aggression this may include management training, assertion training and individual therapy.

Dr Burnett explained to me that the residents are gradually encouraged to accept a great deal of responsibility for their own behaviour. They can earn access to an increasingly large amount of ground leave, town leave and other privileges such as ward outings. He admits that this type of rehabilitation can be 'a slow progress with occasional set-backs'. It culminates, however, in the individual moving on to the open rehabilitation ward. And afterwards? When I next meet Dr Bowden, I do not think that I shall be able to present him with success statistics from St Andrew's. To be honest, I do not attach unlimited significance to statistics of that kind. I can only record my conviction that lasting benefit is obtained by the great majority of the patients.

Kristina Downing-Orr

St Antony's College, Oxford

Kristina Downing-Orr has studied at Boston College, London University, Cambridge University (where she took an M.Phil.) and at Oxford where she is now continuing her invaluable research into juvenile crime and young offenders.

LORD LONGFORD: Talking of young offenders, I understand that you interviewed two hundred young people – a hundred in London and another hundred in Sydney, Australia. What was the common factor?

KRISTINA DOWNING-ORR: They were all homeless. I define homelessness by the way they define themselves. They called themselves homeless, but there are many definitions of homelessness.

LL: Were there some obvious differences between those in Australia and those in England?

KDO: Not so many. The emerging themes from the British side proved to be similar in both cases: a background of physical – including sexual – abuse; disturbed family background or actual broken home.

LL: How many would the former apply to?

KDO: 75 per cent of the female sample had been sexually abused, usually by a member of the family. Reported instances from the male side were not so high – about 40 per cent. In Australia, over half had suffered from physical and sexual abuse and a disruptive family background.

LL: We are talking of both? What counts as family breakdown?

143

Anything other than a normal nuclear family? Breakdown where there is a second marriage? What proportion had quarrelled with their family or a parent?

KDO: Three-quarters at some stage in their lives; that was a big problem. A lot because of general family problems, the presence of a step-father, for instance. Some had been thrown out.

LL: They either left voluntarily or were thrown out?

KDO: Speaking very broadly there were the same factors in both groups although separated by thousands of miles.

LL: Did you look into the question of how many had been in care?

KDO: Half the samples had been in care – either total care or in foster homes.

LL: What proportion had been in trouble with the law?

KDO: Again about half.

LL: So if we are talking about young offenders, these must be typical.

KDO: Yes, but the British sample were not very active in crime. Crime includes prostitution – but they did not regard that as a crime. Their idea was that if sex was going to come into it, they might as well be paid. This applied mainly, of course, to those who had been sexually abused in childhood.

Another interesting thing I found was that with prostitution and drug addiction, a component of self-esteem appeared to be tied up with it. The more dangerous the drug, the greater the degree of self-esteem involved. This was a part of their life; if their life was down in the sewer, as it was for a lot of them, the way to use self-esteem was to have to contend with the more difficult and vile components, with drugs. If someone was addicted to speed, that did not carry the same street credibility associated with heroin. In Britain, I found that the drug of choice was not heroin but marijuana or LSD – by and large, marijuana. The sample in Britain was much less deviant than the sample in Australia.

LL: You say that half of these young people had been in trouble with the law.

KDO: The justification they had was that they did not do actual harm to anybody. They only mugged people who they thought had money; only broke into the houses of people who they considered were well off, where they were covered by insurance. The argument was, 'I am not taking anything from anybody who is going to miss it.'

144

LL: What age are we talking about?

KDO: 16 to 21.

LL: Would you say they had a moral code of their own?

KDO: Yes, there was certainly a moral code, but a rather strange moral code. They did not regard themselves as deviant.

LL: They would not see themselves as nutters?

KDO: Definitely not. They viewed themselves in both places as a family – a family that argued a lot, maybe. They would say that they did not steal from one another, but of course they did. They shared a moral code and did support each other – if somebody, or the public, were attacking them, for example. They would often share what money or food they had and would look after each other.

LL: I did not realize there was a sort of family feeling. We are talking about young offenders – some of them had been in trouble with the law. Had any of them actually been in prison?

KDO: Yes, a lot of them. They felt that while in prison they learnt to be professional criminals. They went in as amateurs. Many had been introduced to drugs while in prison.

LL: How can young people who misbehave be helped? What are the alternatives to custody? Some of them must have been on probation – did that do them any good?

KDO: The homeless issue is the one to approach. Life for the homeless can be very rough. It affects people in so many ways. They can't handle the tensions. They mug out of frustration; they take to violence because of the frustration in their lives. They turn to drink and this causes them to be even more violent.

LL: When they break probation, does that mean anything to them?

KDO: They have not really stressed that too much. There have been quite a few on probation, but that does not affect them very much. One interesting thing was their jaded perceptions of the criminal justice system. One young man said that he had broken into a shop and stolen £400. He was fined £20 – but did not have to give up the £400.

LL: What do you feel about the treatment of these young people when they break the law?

KDO: The prison system is a pack of anachronisms. While I think that the public must be protected from people who have committed

145

violent crimes, there does not seem to be much of an instructional or rehabilitative nature applied in prison.

LL: If you kill somebody, you must be punished. You will agree that people who commit crimes should be punished? How otherwise can you maintain law and order?

KDO: Surely there should be therapy and rehabilitation?

LL: But what about law and order?

KDO: My young people commit a crime and don't think about what will happen to them as a result. I don't think putting them in prison with adult prisoners is at all a good idea – or in approved school, for that matter. Give them some education and provide them with some life skills; they have no social skills, no life skills, and no self-esteem except in dealing with crime. It is not enough just to lock them up. Before you can solve a problem, you have to seek the cause and treat the symptoms. If you don't know what the cause is, you won't be able to solve the problem. It seems to me that there is very little done in prisons to ensure that there will not be a repetition of the offence.

LL: Broken homes are great causes of crime.

KDO: It is a serious problem. Not all my young people came from broken homes or had working-class backgrounds. There were some middle-class cases – especially in Australia – and this had far-reaching ramifications. How is the National Health Service treating family conflict? A lot of my youngsters came from families where there was a lot of violence – there should be more facilities to help these young people. Those who have been in care, for example, are released onto the streets when they reach 16 or so and nothing more is done for them.

LL: What kind of help can be given to them? The New Horizon Youth Centre helps them in many ways – puts them in touch with social services, supports them in court, provides shelter, warmth and social amenities.

KDO: Places like New Horizon are great, it is true. There are lots of little projects, such as the Little Red School in Norfolk, a Danish project over here. They work with and have done a lot for young people, delinquents.

LL: When you meet these young people, do you ask them what went wrong?

KDO: We have a tendency to label them as delinquent and this isolates them from other people. They respond accordingly. They are still children – a lot of them are frightened, terrified in fact.

LL: But they may have done some terrible things.

KDO: In a perfect world, I would like them to be given some therapeutic counselling.

LL: Are they ready to receive that? What about a psychiatrist?

KDO: It can be very scary for young people to be put into psycho-analysis. It is not necessarily therapeutic.

LL: Could you help them with hypnotherapy?

KDO: There are lots of layers of self-protection – they have a lot of layers of defence mechanisms. They need them to survive. Those layers have to be chipped away, and if you were just to provide counselling services, very few people would come. But if they had a supportive environment, like that at New Horizon, they could ident-ify with the workers; if they get to know somebody, it is different. Some spoke to me, for example, for three hours and did not want to stop talking. It is important to be non-judgemental in dealing with them. These problems are going to be with us a long time.

LL: It is difficult to be non-judgemental about stealing, or violence. Do you try to alter their attitude?

KDO: The people who need the most help often don't get it because they are violent.

LL: But how do you help them? You think by counselling? Would the counsellors need special training?

KDO: It must be psychological therapy. Hypnosis is therapeutic and is powerful stuff. You have to start somewhere and in places where people feel comfortable and not threatened. A lot of the issues these young people face are frightening, and I don't think it can be healthy if it is all boxed up inside them. It is going to repeat itself. We should provide life skills, ordinary skills. I found that New Horizon provided a place where these young people could get off the streets, keep warm in winter and where they felt comfortable. They learnt to trust the workers and that is a good point. I would like to see it taken one step further.

LL: You would like a therapist on the staff at places like New Horizon?

KDO: Yes, that's right. I think that is very important. There is always the danger that somebody would not wish to be seen going to a therapist, but some of them told me things they would have talked to a therapist about.

LL: Do you think anything could be done to unite them with their families?

KDO: Quite a few had run away from home several times. So that does not seem to be a good idea.

LL: But what about those who had been in care? They would presumably return to their families.

KDO: Half of my samples have spent some time in care, and local authorities are not doing enough to ensure that these young people steer clear of trouble subsequently.

Baroness Faithfull of Wolvercote

Former Director of Social Services, Oxford

An outstanding contributor to debates in the House of Lords, Lucy Faithfull is President of the National Children's Bureau, Vice-President of Barnardo's, and an Honorary Member of the Council of the NSPCC, among many other duties – and all this after a lifetime's work in health and child care which included being Director of Social Services for Oxford.

LORD LONGFORD: Should youngsters be treated differently from adult offenders?

LADY FAITHFULL: When I was Director of Social Services, if an order was made for a child to be removed from home and come into the care of the local authority, the order might come through the court because the child had committed an offence or it might come from the social services for reasons such as a death in the family or the mother being unable to cope. We did not separate the two types of child. Over the 18 years I worked for Oxford City Council, first as a Children's Officer and later as Director of Social Services, we only had three children sent to approved schools.

LL: You sent them there because they were impossible to cope with?

LF: Well, the court did. If the court made a recommendation, you had to comply whether you agreed with it or not. There are some children who are so disturbed that they need therapeutic treatment. Those I would send away to the Caldecott Community, for instance, which gives special therapeutic treatment.

LL: You were not punishing them?

149

LF: No, but we have to be careful as it is 15 years since I was *en poste*. I am told that children these days are far more difficult to deal with than they were in my day. Take what is going on now in Liverpool, Bristol and even in Oxford – on the Blackbird Leys Estate, for example. Whether my principles would work now, I don't know.

I have to say that the social services now, compared with my day, are at a great disadvantage because their resources have been cut. Moreover, the concept of social services nowadays is quite different from what it used to be. When I was working, social services consisted of what we then called case work, which implied a personal relationship between the social workers and the children we dealt with. Today the social services organize their work by putting it out to voluntary organizations or even to private enterprise.

LL: What is the Caldecott Community? Is it voluntary?

LF: The Caldecott Community – I am on the board – is for deeply disturbed children. I am also a governor of a place called Bessels Leigh, which is a school dealing with educationally very disturbed children. One of the problems today is that therapeutic residential care centres are very expensive and, as a consequence, city treasurers no longer allow children to go to them, even if they need to. They say that it costs too much and the local authority can't afford it.

Again, a large number of EBD schools, which used to be called schools for maladjusted children, now come under the umbrella of the Department of Education. They are for educationally disturbed children and are having to close because local authorities are not prepared to send children to them on account of the expense. A lot of children who get into trouble later on would not have done so if they had been able to benefit from these facilities. I am running a campaign about this at the moment.

LL: When we talk of children and young people, who are you thinking of?

LF: We are talking about everyone up to 18 – they now go out of care at 18.

LL: The younger half of the young offenders?

LF: Well, it depends what you are looking at. I maintain that a lot of these children at Feltham would not be there if they had been given the proper treatment at an earlier stage. One of our problems is that we are not giving children the help they need at an early enough stage, either under the Education Act of 1981 or under the Children Act of 1989. When I say helping the children, I must stress that you can't help children unless you help families.

150

LL: The point you are making is that if only you could treat these people young enough, they would not turn out the way they do.

LF: Yes, but a number of other factors come into it as well. I do wonder these days – the new breed of social services directors are not trained social workers, they are just managers.

LL: I still thought they were case workers.

LF: Since the Seebohm Report which came into implementation in 1970, social workers have got so much to do and are ill-equipped to do it. They only have two years' training. On the Continent, in France and Germany, they have three or four years' training. Our social workers have got so much more to do now. This is terribly important at the moment. The new concept of local authority social work is that directors of social services should be managers. They organize the work and, for instance, when they find they have not got enough old people's homes, they contact various voluntary organizations and make a contract with them, instead of running their own old people's homes. When I was Director of Social Services, I had seven old people's homes for which I was responsible. But that is not the case now.

LL: You can't know them all personally.

LF: This concept of a personal relationship with your cases is not widely held now, though it may still be held in some areas. But our social workers don't get the kind of training that they should.

LL: Where can I see some kind of training?

LF: They hold a very good course in Oxford. Talking of Oxford, we are very worried about Bessels Leigh School. It is having difficulty now in finding enough children to keep going, because the local authority say they cannot afford to pay for them. We are cutting off our noses to spite our faces by cutting back on social policies which in the end prove to be more expensive. I maintain that all the problems at the moment are due to the fact that our back-up services for childhood have not been good enough. That goes not only for the social services, but equally so for education and therapeutic treatment. A very great number of child guidance clinics have closed down, which is really serious. In the past it was always possible to refer difficult children to a clinic, where they worked in teams of three – a social worker, a psychologist and a psychiatrist, representing the Department of Health, the Home Office and the social services. The position now is that because of the shortage of social workers, who have been withdrawn to meet demands elsewhere, the teams

151

have been disbanded and the clinics forced to close. A great deal of good work is being done by voluntary organizations, but local authority social services have been so cut down that their work with children has diminished.

Another example: I used to go to Grendon Underwood, the psychiatric prison, and talk to the men when they were about to be discharged. I used to go in the evening at about eight o'clock. The men wanted to see me, in order to know how they should treat their children when they went back home – should they tell the children that they had committed an offence and been sent to prison? I often spent two or three hours with them and nearly always it used to come back to the fact that if they had had somebody to help them when they were young, they would not have been at Grendon. Among all these citizen's charters today, there is no charter for children. They have left children out and until the community, until the schools and until the social workers actually work together, we shall continue to have trouble.

LL: The worst children tend to come from the worst homes, and they are not homes that are going to hand their children over to therapists and suchlike.

LF: When I was working in Oxford, the Barton Estate was as bad as any estate in this country. We used to arrange for the children to attend clinics and sometimes we would send them away to a thera- peutic centre. I can say they really benefited and came back very much better in every way. All that side of social work is going.

The trouble is that nobody carries responsibility. If you write to the ministry, they say that it is the local authority's business; if you go to the local authority, they say that they are rate-capped and have not got the resources.

LL: Coming now to the new Criminal Justice Act – do you approve of it? In theory it is going to be harder to send young people to penal custody. The government are apparently not ready to say that young people of 15 won't go to penal custody, but they are ready to discuss the time when that might happen. But then the question arises: What do you do with young people in their teens who have done terrible things like rape – young boys of 15, too young for penal custody?

LF: Sex offenders like that should be treated, not sent to prison. I profoundly believe that either prisons should be run differently or the men should have therapeutic treatment in the community. There are people who say that the men have done wrong and should be punished – but that does not get you anywhere. Our prison services

152

are so awful as to be past belief. Of course, you do have to put people in prison to safeguard society, but we would do far better if we treated the people in prison in a different way.

LL: I want to press you on this particular point. If you take young people under 18, enlightened people say they should not go to penal custody. Do you think the social services are capable of treating them? Who is really going to be able to deal with youngsters who have committed very serious crimes?

LF: It is no good giving help to children only – you have got to be in touch with and supporting the parents. Places like Barnardo's and the National Children's Homes are running these family centres. I visited a family centre run by Barnardo's. There were about 30 women. They come for the day, with their children. They learn to cook, to sew, receive counselling. They talk about their problems with their husbands, enjoy the companionship with each other and so on. We need to develop this kind of thing much more. And then, of course, there is the question of the community – the community counts as well.

LL: Take youngsters under 18 who come before the new Youth Courts, when they have done dreadful things. People say they should not be sent to custody. Do you see any future in secure units actually staffed by social workers? I think myself that probation officers would be better at it, but they are not at all keen on that sort of thing. It really comes down to local authorities providing the facilities.

LF: I feel very sad about this, because there used to be remand homes run on friendly therapeutic lines. In each remand home there was a secure unit. I remember one example – we had a child who had murdered his mother. He was put in a secure unit and the local curate used to come in each night and sleep in the room next to the unit. You see, they have closed all these remand homes.

LL: I have visited a lot of children's homes, but they were all staffed by unqualified workers. Do you think such people are really capable of dealing with these difficult offenders?

LF: Here again, you have put your finger on it. I am always having a battle over the training of social workers. In the old remand home in Oxford, run by Oxford County, all the staff were trained and the head was a trained social worker. In all my children's homes in Oxford, we had trained staff. In Oxford now, they are thinking of closing, or curtailing, the hospital for disturbed, unhappy children. Can you believe it?

Dr John Rae

Former Headmaster, Westminster School

Most of Dr John Rae's adult life has been spent in education. Before taking over the headmastership of Westminster School, which he held from 1970 to 1986, he had spells at Harrow and at Taunton School. He was also a magistrate for four years.

LORD LONGFORD: What causes young people to become offenders?

JOHN RAE: Speaking as a citizen, rather than an educationalist, I think that some people may inherit and develop traits of character that make them more inclined to break the law, some develop traits that make them less inclined.

LL: Inherited?

JR: Inherited traits but also developed by living and upbringing. Some will never commit offences, whatever problems they face, while others, whatever the circumstances, will bend or break laws.

LL: You were in charge of boys from the well-to-do classes – do you think that made a difference?

JR: Among the hundreds or thousands of boys I came across during my teaching years, I found as much diversity of character as you would find in any social group of young adolescents. The inclination to break the law may be in all of us. If some boys were put into different socio-economic circumstances, they would have been criminals from talent or opportunity. What influences them away from breaking the law is the upbringing developed by family and school, and because they don't need to break the law.

154

LL: Do you mean breaking school rules, such as no smoking, or breaking the law?

JR: The rule-breaker is not an embryonic law-breaker – it is natural to try to kick over traces, particularly in adolescence, and it is comparatively unusual never to try to break rules. But there is also another category, the pupil that breaks not the school rules but the law of the land.

LL: Drugs?

JR: Illicit drugs, yes, and stealing, not only within school but in local shops. That sort of dishonesty, stealing, occurs more often among pupils of affluent background than the outside world realizes.

LL: I recall an instance when four boys were expelled for that at Eton.

JR: This is something which has not changed. These are people who are quite prepared to break not just the rules but the law as well. What I conclude from that in the first place is that people are inclined to break the law if circumstances encourage it – perhaps more people than we realize. If inhibiting factors – parents, school, expulsion, public punishment – do not operate, then breaking the law is relatively common or easy.

Second, I have to make one sexist comment. The girls only came to Westminster in the 6th form at 16 and I cannot think of a single case where I knew for certain they broke the law of the land. They broke school rules, yes, wore wrong clothes ... little things.

I believe adolescence has a direct connection with rule-breaking and law-breaking. Because the girls came later, after adolescence, they were less likely to break the law. So a critical time as to whether an individual will go down the criminal path lies in adolescence. Comparatively few men, if they put their hands on their heart and were asked, 'Have you ever broken the law of the land?', would be able to answer 'no'. Perhaps they stole Mars Bars, cheated on rail tickets, that sort of thing.

For pupils in a school, whether private or State schools, breaking the rules is normal, I would say healthy. Somebody who never breaks a single school rule is not abnormal or ill, but he or she is unusual. It is a testing of authority. Those going a little further often don't regard it a serious immoral decision. Some may explain it as a cry for attention, but I would take the view that they do it for kicks, the thrill of getting away with it, and for the obvious reason of wanting something they can't afford.

Low-level criminality in adolescence is widespread in all social classes and should not be considered foreign to basic instinct. Those who live in less well-structured families, or who are less inclined to worry about social disgrace, may start sooner and continue longer.

LL: So you would say that in adolescence there is a tendency to break the law?

JR: It's an attempt to kick against the traces. Very little explanation is needed – young men in particular try to assert themselves. If that wasn't the case, they would never grow up. The danger is that adult authority keels over too quickly, and lets them get away with it.

LL: I am amazed with all your experience to hear you say that.

JR: At the age of 11 I was at boarding school, during the war when there was sweet rationing, and a group of us stole sweets from a local shop. Two of us distracted the shop-keeper, two knocked the sweets off into our pockets. We were caught and beaten, never did it again. We were all middle class, pre-adolescent, we never did it again, but we certainly did it. There was no criminal record but our parents were informed.

This raises an important point, I think, that in independent schools these problems are usually dealt with by the school. It never needs to go to the police and courts. Which raises the question why most boys who are expelled do not go on to a life of criminality. What part did the fact that they weren't in the hands of the law play? Is it better metaphorically to cuff them on the ear rather than bring in the strong arm of the law?

LL: Were many boys caught?

JR: Not that many, probably the tip of the iceberg. Things got lost, went astray, some weren't reported. It wasn't rife, but common enough. Other headmasters and headmistresses would agree. Some say sadly that this is all too common and they would argue about a materialistic society. These boys are not in want at all.

LL: We do these things at public schools and are dealt with at source.

JR: It certainly is worth thinking about, that these boys and girls who break the law are dealt with by their own community and on the whole don't pursue a life of crime. It may be coincidental – better home support, better moral training – but it could be connected. I once did some amateur research – a survey – to see whether there was a correlation between broken homes and the likelihood of getting into trouble. There was no correlation.

LL: I did an enquiry for Nuffield into young offenders and the only evidence we came up with was a possible relationship – not a causal factor.

JR: It could be there are so many broken homes now that that factor is not so significant. Another factor, in a sense, is the unimportance of what adolescents do. If what they do is held against them subsequently, which of us would escape whipping?

I am not proposing this as a practical solution, but I do suggest that independent schools who deal with their own trouble means that your slate is wiped clean at 18. Whatever you've done, it's been paid for; you can't do that with young offenders, but I believe it is useful for petty crimes.

LL: The Dartington Social Research Unit would reach the same conclusion. There was a case of a young fellow of 17 who murdered someone because he wanted to know what it was like to kill.

JR: That is the important distinction – the most extreme violence wouldn't be found in a public school. They would be sacked before they got that far. I think the adolescent in more affluent circumstances nevertheless goes through a period when he is likely to break the rules of the school and may well break the law of the land in what may be regarded as a minor way – smoking cannabis, stealing, public transport offences; but not physical violence, breaking and entering, not carrying a knife, behaving like a lager lout or football thug.

LL: Like the riot in Thornton Heath by children?

JR: You won't find gang warfare that leads to real violence in public schools. They may have the same racial prejudice and tend to run in gangs, but they won't hit somebody with iron bars and clubs. There are some factors in common and some inhibiting factors.

LL: If you were asked to compare Westminster with a good comprehensive school, would the comprehensive school be more in line with Westminster or with a poor comprehensive school?

JR: In some senses a good comprehensive, away from the inner city, could have even better behaviour than a public school. Whatever inhibiting factor it is that restrains normal adolescents from becoming habitual criminals exists in public and independent schools alike and may come from within the family, but reinforced by schools.

LL: Is there any special view you have of what ought to be done?

JR: I was a juvenile magistrate at one stage before becoming a headmaster. I don't think there is a magic wand, but the independent schoolboy does have so many opportunities to release energy – games are not irrelevant to this, because the whole international world of sport has its origins in public schools trying to avoid boys acting like offenders. In the early nineteenth century, many schools were faced with violence and anarchy, and many games grew up to stop boys acting like thugs.

The provision of well-organized facilities and opportunities would also improve the problem. I don't know what you do with young men intent on going down the criminal route. In custody they could become habitual criminals. But society will always face a problem, particularly with male adolescents. In previous centuries, life was brutal and often adolescents were badly treated; there's no magic wand.

LL: You mean boys who might become thugs and begin to threaten the elderly or vulnerable?

JR: To women, the young and the elderly, these aggressive adolescents are very threatening. Societies that somehow manage to contain this adolescent aggression tend to be totalitarian – Hitler Youth and so on. If you dragoon all adolescents into youth movements that are very aggressive it allows legitimate thuggery. The Young Pioneers in the Soviet Union are another example.

LL: Did Westminster have boxing lessons?

JR: Boxing was not allowed, but we may have to return to it as a possible solution. There are dangers in boxing, but it might be a good thing to help the controlled and organized use of aggression rather than have it left loose.

The majority of adolescents get into trouble of a comparatively minor sort. I fear the present system may be sucking in the majority of offenders because the minority need custodial sentences and are really dangerous and threatening. Society's anxiety about the minority may extend the punishment to the majority.

LL: Most enlightened people want adolescents kept out of prison. At Feltham, I went to an Open Day where the address was given by a lady whose son was bullied to death there.

JR: I feel we have probably confused enlightenment with indulgence: some young people do benefit from the adult world taking a consistently tough line, and some problems with young offenders arise because adult life is so wet and confused and unwilling to say 'no, that's enough'. In good schools the boys, particularly, have been in a controlled situation from 8 years old at least and have grown up

158

in an environment where no means no and yes and means yes. If children are brought up to have their own way from babyhood, it's much more difficult to impose self-discipline.

The Rt Rev. Robert Hardy

The Bishop of Lincoln

The Bishop of Lincoln is styled 'Minister to Prisons'. No one discussing these matters with him can doubt his first-hand knowledge of prison and prisoners. I must pass over many aspects of his ministry, including his chairmanship of two major conferences on prisons, and I will confine myself to a thesis written by himself and a colleague. It may be thought, after reading Chapter 7 of the thesis, that the suggestions made for dealing with such practical problems as vandalism, shop-lifting and football hooliganism, while entirely laudable, are not different in kind from suggestions that might emanate from public-spirited Humanists. Again, the advice that he gives to well-intentioned parishioners could be paralleled from outside the Churches.

What is distinctive, however, in his witness is summarized in Chapter 6, under the heading 'What has Christianity to Say?'. To put the question in his own way, 'At the practical level we must consider whether Christians have anything distinctive to say about a particular moral problem, in our case the problem of delinquency.' He passes quickly over the Christian devotion to prayer, worship and church-going. He does not claim any advantage, though it may well be that he believes that one exists for the Christian profession of the Holy Spirit. He boldly sets out the essential message that

Christian morality proceeds from a distinctive base – the idea that while we are yet sinners Christ died for us. From this statement and example of self-giving love, Christian morality is worked out as a response to any given situation. Indeed, it is through his response that the individual Christian attempts to find a path which reflects the love that God has shown him. Other moralities, besides the Christian, attempt to find the moral way. But the Christian approach brings a unity to moral behaviour, because it relates

160

it to God and his love, as shown us in Jesus Christ. It is this which makes Christian morality a morality of response. It is a response to the God who is to be identified with the good, not merely as an idea, but embodied in a human life-story, that of Jesus of Nazareth.

Does this response to God inspire the Christian to be any special ethical quality? The Bishop of Lincoln has no doubt about the answer to that question. He finds a special Christian virtue in agape. 'It is important,' he continues, 'to note that a Christian regards agape, self-giving love, as distinctive because of his or her standpoint of faith.' How then, he asks, can agape be applied to the problems of delinquency? He proposes four elements which may well provide us with a useful set of pointers for discovering what Christians have to say. Of these, only the first can be described as having a content which could not be shared by a sensitive Humanist. The other three can only be indicated here. Agape involves a careful balancing act between the appropriate love for society and the individual. Although we allow for the immaturity of delinquents, we refuse to treat them as entirely lacking in responsibility. Agape means a sacrificial giving of oneself in whatever context it is exercised. But what is most interesting for our purposes is the first of the Bishop's four pointers, the one not likely to be shared by Humanists. The first application of agape, he tells us, involves assessing the problem of delinquency within the overall context of God's love for mankind. This means that if we care for the delinquent, or for the problem of delinquency, our care is to be set in the widest possible context of the love of God for his creation – for men and women and children.

Father Gerald Ennis
Former Prison Chaplain

Father Gerald Ennis was a Catholic prison chaplain for 14 years. He retired in 1990 from Feltham Young Offenders' Institution. He is now AIDS Pastoral Care Co-ordinator for the Diocese of Worcester.

LORD LONGFORD: Looking back over your very varied experience, do you feel that people under 21 should be treated differently by the courts?

FATHER GERALD ENNIS: I suppose the age of 21 is an arbitrary line that people draw. There's certainly a case for making a special effort to be more positive in the custody of young people. Crime is a pastime for relatively young men. Very often, when you see someone in an adult institution over the age of 40, it's a surprise. You need to get to youngsters before they are convinced they themselves have no future as a law-abiding citizen.

I believe very strongly that every person working in a prison, whatever discipline, has to aim to give offenders a better understanding of their own dignity and importance, their own worth. A priest, particularly, has the task of convincing youngsters and adults that there is something unique about them. The trouble is that they have grown up with the constant reminder that they are not worth anything; they've been told so, believe it, and act accordingly.

LL: I believe you took Mother Teresa into Wormwood Scrubs?

GE: We had the Missionaries of Charity coming into prison on Saturdays and one day they told me that Mother Teresa was going to see them when she was shuttling between London and Northern Ireland. She had about an hour and a half with us. She addressed

162

the heads of departments at the morning meeting and stressed the responsibilities that people with power had. As usual, she got everyone on their feet to pray. After that she attended Mass in the Chapel and then addressed the prisoners. Many men in the congregation had life sentences and her message was that they had an enormous amount to accept but at the same time they had an awful lot to offer.

LL: You were mentioning the importance of developing self-esteem before prisoners become too hardened.

GE: I think that's why training is so vital. If they can acquire a skill in prison, that helps self-esteem. If they can develop physically or learn to read and write, do exams – all these things are part of building self-esteem. At Feltham the general picture is that there are hardly any opportunities at all. Why can't any be produced? Everything depends on having enough disciplined staff to ensure youngsters go to classes.

LL: You wouldn't claim Feltham has gone very far in direction of your ideal?

GE: There's been a deterioration in the regime. It's a sad fact that while having a successful governor, conditions got worse. A lot more was done before Fresh Start. Fresh Start was a good idea but the Treasury hijacked it into a penny-pinching exercise.

LL: I understand that when you were at Feltham there was no bullying. It has come in recently?

GE: I wasn't conscious of a great deal of bullying. We knew certain youngsters were vulnerable because they were small or weak. They'd have tobacco or canteen goods taken under threat. It was always a feature, but not in the way it is today. If you haven't enough staff, prison may become a jungle.

LL: On the spiritual side, what do you feel you can contribute that ordinary lay staff can't?

GE: The State can feed, exercise, train – that's no more than running a dogs' home. Who has the spiritual input that makes a person what he is? The chaplain should be an important member of management in that he is *par excellence* the conscience of the system.

Most people feel that they have no responsibility for what happens in prisons, for what the regime is and the fabric of the buildings. Brixton, for example, is an appalling scandal.

LL: Will prisoners confide in a chaplain?

GE: All confidences depend on relationships. Some chaplains might not have that as much as a landing officer. On the other hand, someone may see the chaplain as a friend because he isn't in a uniform. A chaplain can only engage a prisoner who wants to talk to him. In the 14 years that I was a prison chaplain, never once when I put my key in the door, knocked on the cell door and opened it, did I get a rejection – they'd say yes. In the AIDS unit I now visit I was told three times in two months by a registered Roman Catholic that he didn't want to talk to me. I think the Church has constantly shown a more positive attitude to prisoners than to gay men. To be a practising gay is to break rules. We all break rules. God doesn't punish sin by sickness.

LL: If you get through to a gay man, what is your message?

GE: He's a precious in the sight of God. Every single one of us is made in God's image and likeness, redeemed by Christ. We fail when someone feels that the Church has nothing to offer them.

LL: And your work with prisoners has helped you to deliver this message?

GE: It has certainly been a good preparation. I have been very conscious of the great privilege it's been to be a prison chaplain, because it's out of the heart of the Gospel, Christ's love for sinners and love for the weak and exploited. Many, many times I've experienced the goodness of people in prison. Men there have taught me more than books.

LL: Coming to a different aspect – should custody be much reduced for young people?

GE: I believe that prisons should be used simply to protect the public. This may well be naive, I don't know. The community needs protection; anyone who is a threat should be out of circulation. But anyone who is not a threat to society should not be in prison.

LL: Where should young people go, if not to prison, when they have committed serious crimes?

GE: They should go to prison to protect society. But most young offenders are in for thefts, house-breaking, car stuff. I honestly don't know the answer. Serious questions need to be asked of what we do by locking people up. I don't think we've ever thought through what prison does. Relatively speaking, prison is a new phenomenon. In transportation days, Australia was the most law-abiding Western society within one generation of deportation. That tells us about the good that can be done without taking away a person's liberty.

164

LL: Take joy-riding. Should it just continue?

GE: I don't feel that prison is right. Nobody has ever looked at the effect of prison from a theological point of view. Man is made in the image of God and this means he has been given the ability to choose. Imprisonment takes away that characteristic of ours that is like God. Much more damaging than flogging, not necessarily more civilized. No one has thought it through. I'm not advocating corporal punishment, but it's just as damaging to lock someone up. Psychiatrists and psychologists say that after five years in custody you are irrevocably scarred.

Cardinal Hume came to Wormwood Scrubs B Wing one Christmas, where there were 600 boys waiting reallocation. The Cardinal said that he was left with a striking contrast between Ampleforth School and Wormwood Scrubs. One was a community of privilege, one of underprivilege. He though it an accident of birth.

LL: Do you feel that life in a young offenders' prison could be more effective?

GE: The more resources you have, the less harmful the effects of confinement are. If you had tremendous inner resources you'd survive, but without them you need outside resources. You're dealing here with people who are inadequate in ordinary life. They can't improve without help from beyond themselves.

LL: What will happen to these young people? They could benefit from guidance. A special religious approach?

GE: In the old days we did have religious orders running Borstals, and in approved schools there were Salesians, Christian Brothers and so on. They had strong disciplinarian structures. The young people hated it. There was a lot of beating.

Before I left Westminster Cathedral 20 years ago, I was in charge of a youth club. I found it far easier to be a prison chaplain than run a youth club because in prison the youngsters have clearly defined limits. They know exactly how far they can go before the sanctions come. Youngsters need to know that if they go over the boundary there will be swift retribution. There should be clear demarcation lines before it gets to the stage of prison – it starts with the family. If you're secure and know the boundaries, that will support you. I had very firm lines of demarcation as a child but I was loved and valued.

When I was working as a prison chaplain I often said to them, 'I'm the only person in this place who can give you a free pardon!' If God has given you the assurance of forgiveness through your

Christian ministry, you must ask yourself whether you have the right to withhold forgiveness. God's forgiveness is always there; a third party can reveal forgiveness – perhaps the victim. The last person to exercise forgiveness is the man himself.

Lord Hunt of Llanfair Waterdine

Former Chairman of the Parole Board

From 1956 to 1966, Lord Hunt was the first Director of the Duke of Edinburgh's Award Scheme for young people. From 1967 to 1974 he was the first Chairman of the Intermediate Treatment Fund which supported many schemes for young people to find a form of self-expression other than through crime.

John Hunt will go down in history, of course, as the leader of the first team to climb Mount Everest. It was typical of him that he sent on two of his team, one of them Edmund Hillary, to attain the summit. Mountaineering has been one of the major inspirations of his life, but even more so has been the whole concept of moral leadership. For John Hunt, a leader's place is 'not in front, but in the middle'.

I should make it clear that what follows are Lord Hunt's written answers to the questions that I put to him.

LORD LONGFORD: What has been your experience of juvenile crime?

LORD HUNT: The perusal of a massive documentation of cases considered for parole during my chairmanship – we considered some 5,000 cases a year – showed how many inmates serving three years or more for serious offences had started their careers of crime as juveniles, serving in approved schools, proceeding to custody in detention centres, Borstal, and adult imprisonment. We had regular contacts with the police, probation and social services and with magistrates, as well as visiting prisons. All these visits gave us further insight into juvenile crime an its origins.

LL: Are too many young offenders sent to penal custody?

JH: It is now the policy of the government to keep as many young offenders as possible out of custody. There are several stages in implementing that policy:

1. By police cautioning. This is normal practice with juveniles under 14. It is also used by most police forces for the majority of young offenders aged 14–16. The government is now encouraging an increased use of cautioning among young people aged 17–21.

2. By referral of young offenders to intermediate treatment schemes by the social or probation services.

3. By referral of more serious young offenders to intensive intermediate treatment schemes.

4. By community service orders, which can be applied to 16 years (and above).

5. By attendance centre orders.

6. For the very few but very serious offences committed by a small minority of young people who may represent a physical threat to the public, custody – in a secure hostel or a young offender prison (e.g., Aylesbury) – is necessary.

LL: You are a former Chairman of the Intermediate Treatment Fund. Is IT a way forward?

JH: Intermediate treatment originated in the Children and Young Persons Act 1969, which marked a turning away from institutional care or custody towards so-called 'treatment' in the community. The name purported to describe a stage between a probation order and some form of residential order.

During the 1970s, a number of national voluntary bodies experimented with IT, but its use was patchy, and different standards were applied. It became clear that a nation-wide development, and oversight of standards, would be necessary. In 1978 the DHSS invited the Rainer Foundation to operate such a scheme with funds from that Department, making grants to well-founded programmes in England and Wales. A committee was set up, 50 per cent of whose members were nominated by the Department, the other fifty per cent by invitation of the Rainer Foundation. The IT Fund Committee's first Chairman was Michael King, son of Cecil King, the newspaper publisher. I was President of the Rainer Foundation and, following Mr King's death, took over the chairmanship of the ITF.

I believe that IT has been a success story. The Committee has grant-aided some 100 schemes annually, from many more applications. We kept a close oversight on those schemes both before and following our grants. The main benefits were the inter-agency co-operation involved, the drawing in of much voluntary adult help

168

and the relationships between young delinquents and individual citizens in the community.

A central feature of many such schemes is that juvenile offenders are able to participate in a range of activities with other young people, as members of the local neighbourhood, and *not* as young offenders.

LL: What about the Probation Service?

JH: The Probation Service has accepted the government's invitation to move centre stage in the arena of non-custodial, community-based forms of punishment (or treatment). It will have a co-ordinating function among all the relevant agencies.

While I think it essential that the Probation Service should retain its direct involvement with young offenders and others at risk, I believe that the long history of the Service, and its fine record ever since, fully justify the government's entrustment of this challenging responsibility to the Probation Service.

LL: Adventure schemes for young people – you have much experience of those. Another way forward?

JH: I chaired a conference at St George's House, Windsor, in 1986 which set up a working party to investigate the value of adventure in motivating young people. The group, under my chairmanship, reported in 1989. *In Search of Adventure* provided striking evidence of the value, not only of 'adventure', but more broadly outdoor education in stimulating awareness of the environment, in the sharing of experiences out of doors among young peer groups and with adults, as well as in providing a challenge in one form or another.

This evidence confirmed my own long experience of the effect of such programmes in helping young people through the period of growing up to become responsible and enterprising young citizens with a number of interests and a set of values.

We recommend that by 1995 every young person in the UK should have the opportunity to take part in adventurous outdoor activities.

LL: If the Prime Minister asked you how best to deal with young offenders, what would you say?

JH: I believe that the education and training of our youth, in a society which places great store on materialistic values and whose citizens are so largely motivated by self-interest, is deficient in instilling a sense of caring for others' needs, and a sense of responsibility in that respect. I believe that the initiation of youth to adult status

169

should include a period of service which would embrace all young people at some stage in their lives after leaving full-time education, and before the age of 21.

In ending National Military Service (in the late 1950s) an opportunity was missed to continue and widen that national duty, so as to embrace a wide variety of forms of service within local communities, or further afield.

A decade or more ago, Youth Call and the Tawney Society campaigned actively for such a scheme; but it was deemed to be too costly and politically inexpedient. Today, I fancy that the mood among the voting public might be more receptive. As regards young people themselves, an opinion poll taken some five years ago showed an encouraging 69 per cent in favour of such a form of national service.

I believe that a period of, say, 6–9 months, to be served by all at some convenient stage in their lives after the age of 16, would have a most positive effect on young people's attitudes, conduct and sense of responsibility, to the great benefit of the nation at large.

Esther Rantzen

Chairman of Childline

Esther Rantzen is best known as a highly successful television producer and presenter, but she has long been associated with many good causes. In addition to her valuable work with Childline, she has been a member of the National Consumer Council, the Health Education Authority, the Health Visitors' Association and the Spastics Society, as well as a Trustee of the Ben Hardwick Memorial Fund and an Honorary Member of the NSPCC. She is married to the television producer Desmond Wilcox.

LORD LONGFORD: Could you tell me about how you first came to be interested in the area of child abuse?

ESTHER RANTZEN: I was very struck by a particular case that hit the headlines in about 1985. The parents responsible for a little girl who had been found dead had first met at a special school and, I thought, if this means that they were mentally handicapped and were vulnerable, it could be that this child was always at risk. It could be that social services could have kept a special eye open and supported this family.

Then I began to think: I bet the cases we learn about, the ones that hit the headlines or come to the attention of the statutory authorities, are a tiny fraction of the true amount. So I went to Michael Grade, who was then in charge of BBC1, with a particular letter I had about a child, and I said, 'Would you mind considering this for a possible major investigative programme on BBC1?' Michael had been responsible for creating a programme called *Drugwatch* which I had presented – perhaps we could call a new one *Childwatch?* He realized that it was a very important subject and

171

agreed to do it. I warned him it would be painful, but he recognized that.

LL: How did you go about it?

ER: We asked adult viewers of *That's Life* if they had experienced cruelty as children and if they'd take part in a survey. The results were quite horrific. We got 3,000 completed questionnaires in vivid detail describing it all from an adult perspective. It was terribly painful, because you couldn't reach those children – time had taken them away, so all you could read about was the agony of the memories, utterly unhealed, people talking as if it had happened this week. From their descriptions you could see that it gave them far less chance of a happy matrimonial relationship – lots of marital breakdown, lots of alcohol abuse, drug abuse and crime. There seemed to be a very high percentage of respondents, even though most were women.

When we put this testimony on the screen, it was a real eye-opener. Some people have never forgiven me. Some in the political world from time to time accuse me of having invented child abuse, because the message I carried was so strong.

LL: But you only brought it to light. It's really only in the last few years that child abuse has become an issue.

ER: When we were doing interviews with some of the people who completed the questionnaires and agreed to be interviewed for the programmes, although we didn't identify them or show their faces – I'll never forget a 24-year-old girl who could have been really pretty, but she was grossly fat and depressed, put needles in her arms until they became infected, as a sort of punishment. It's quite common. She said she would sit in a corner like a dog, looking at her mother, praying that she would look into her eyes, but she never did – her mother died when the girl was about 10 or 12 and the abuse intensified. She became very, very disturbed, went into care, had all kinds of psychotherapy. She said, 'I had a psychiatrist who was a man, who put me down as a man-hater.' I asked her if he ever found out why she was, and she said no – 'he never asked'.

This would have been some ten years before I interviewed her. In those days, doctors and psychiatrists weren't asking those kinds of questions – I don't think it was part of their agenda.

LL: You must be given the credit for bringing it all to light.

ER: I think that until we did the programme, and launched the Childline Helpline on that programme in October 1986, social workers and child protection agencies had known of the incidents that were reported to them, but I don't think society as a whole knew. People used to say that it happened in East Anglia or wherever, in another part of the country from where they were.

LL: A report on juvenile offenders estimated that perhaps 50 per cent or up to 70 per cent had been abused.

ER: Freud was mistaken to disbelieve his own patients. There have been many attempts to analyse why Freud couldn't face this knowledge, why he rejected what his patients were telling him as fantasy. But my own experience, talking to survivors of abuse, is that it is an attack on a child's soul. Sexual abuse is dirtier and more defiling than physical abuse, it has all the spiritually destructive qualities of emotional cruelty, where you convince the child that it is worthless, that anything that has happened to it is because it is a bad child. That's the most depressing thing I find when talking to survivors, the loneliness of these children. If what we learn about love and trust and loyalty we learn from our parents and those who care for us, and if that becomes betrayal and fear and pain, there's very little chance as we grown up that we can put love and trust and loyalty into practice, because we've never received it.

LL: Do you believe that in quite a high proportion of cases the children enjoy it?

ER: The most ruthless liars are those who commit sexual offences against children. They put all the responsibility on the child, and that is why the child feels so defiled. They will claim, 'The child seduced me' or 'I did it in my sleep'. What I can guarantee is that the child goes through hell and will continue to go through hell, through life, with those memories. When the child talks, he or she becomes a threat, so the perpetrator will frighten that child by various means, by saying things like 'No one will believe you' or 'If you tell anyone Mum will go to prison' or 'I'll strangle your kitten' – I'm taking all these examples from real life – or 'If you didn't want it you wouldn't have got into bed with me'. Paedophiles groom their victims; seduction can take a long time. Compared to physical violence, life-threatening though it may be, these are the reasons why sexual abuse is an attack on the child's soul. That child, in bed with a grandfather, now feels defiled.

LL: Is there a clear line between cuddling, fondling and real abuse?

ER: Yes, I think there's a clear line. You know very well what a child experiences in a safe cuddle, what you're expressing when you cuddle. When my husband cuddles our children they are safe – he is expressing the fact that they are precious, that he loves them, that he cares about their safety. But sexually abused children don't have safe cuddles, the contact to them is always exploited. As a result, when they grow up and have relationships of their own, often the girls will enter into relationships with partners who abuse them.

LL: I have met someone in prison for abusing a younger brother and sisters who was in fact himself abused by his father. Is there much of that?

ER: It does happen. I'm afraid the spiral continues. I have heard from a psychiatrist that abused boys do identify with abusers, whereas abused girls continue the victim mode into their adult lives. Of course, one of the dreadful things is that that's the only way they relate, they've become accustomed to it.

LL: Is abuse more prevalent in the working class?

ER: When we did an opinion poll for the first *Childwatch* programme in 1986, we found child abuse right across the board economically. Physical violence was slightly more common among poorer families and emotional cruelty was more common among the affluent.

LL: Coldness?

ER: I think we've lived through the Dark Ages for children in Britain – that children should be seen and not heard, that babies should be fed on the clock and cuddled as little as possible because you are making a rod for your own back. Look at how our towns are designed – where are the play areas, crèches in shopping precincts, support for mothers breast-feeding? Look at the joy-riding kids – where else is there for them to play?

LL: Is the level of abuse getting worse?

ER: There's no way of telling. It has always been a secret crime, so that it has never been possible to assess real numbers. But as families split and scatter more, with people coming and going, children can be alone in the house, perhaps just with Dad who is at home without a job. We seem to have dislocated family life, and therefore I do fear that children are still marginalized. The safety of children depends on safe, warm relationships with a number of adults, not just on the nuclear family. I had aunts I could talk to, grandparents ... just someone to keep an eye on you, to see if something is going wrong.

LL: Do you think there is a link between abuse and a climate of sexual liberation?

ER: There is a line – paedophiles are different from people who

174

have sex with consenting adults. If we could find the cause of sex offending, it would be wonderful.

LL: Does a sense of power come into it?

ER: Very much. A psychiatrist once told me that findings with her own client-base indicated a link with being bullied. Quite often these are not very confident men, and often her patients told her that when they were having sex with children they would get flashbacks to when they were the victims of gangs or bullies. Maybe it is some sort of vengeful act.

LL: What would you say if the Prime Minister asked for your advice?

ER: Prioritize children, appoint a Minister for Children. Also, once a child has disclosed abuse, that family needs professional support. It may not need it for all that long, but it needs the capacity to talk about the experience in a therapeutic environment – counselling really does help.

LL: How do you help them?

ER: Talking. We need professional counselling support for survivors – the children, the family, everyone. If a husband has been doing it and the mother doesn't know, she will feel guilty, bitter, jealous – 'Was I too little of a woman, not good enough for him?' They need to re-establish a relationship with their daughter, and the daughter needs to have the responsibility taken off her. Make it absolutely clear that it is *his* crime, not hers. It doesn't take long and it is tremendously productive, because what we're working on are the families of tomorrow. If that girl can grow up without repeating the pattern of abuse, we're not only saving the lives of children now but in the future.

Counselling is the growth industry of the future. I wonder if it's a reflection of the loneliness I was talking about before, that people find it very difficult to listen to each other in these hurried times.

LL: Should counsellors be fully trained?

ER: You do need training. They do need to know what they are doing because some survivors are extremely badly damaged and can be dangerous in that they confuse love and hate.

LL: One adolescent waited twelve years to strangle their abuser.

ER: I would see that as self-defence. I think he was criminally assaulted. But you also asked me about liberation. We are coming across evidence that video pornography is being used by sexual offenders to soften up their victims. We're not happy about that.

They use all kinds of pornography in their grooming.

LL: I'm surprised there are no other agencies in this area.

ER: Well, there are – local authority social services are wonderful, as are child protection agencies, but some members of the Establishment are so horrified by these revelations that they just won't take it on board and say that I'm inventing it.

LL: Some children fantasize.

ER: On Childline we have many children phoning anonymously. They don't want to make trouble by naming adults, but they are talking of their own pain and distress. We can very seldom persuade them to ask for help because they are so terrified that intervention can bring catastrophe to their families. They've usually been intimidated that Dad will go to prison or they'll be sent to care, and very often it's true. In these circumstances you can only say that this child is either a Sarah Bernhardt or in desperate distress, because what's in it for her? She isn't telling us who she is or where she is. She's only talking about how it makes her feel.

LL: What of the abused children who stay at home?

ER: What children who ring Childline most fear is that all they have – their home, their brothers and sisters, their Mum – will be taken from them if they ask for help. What they desperately want is for Daddy to stop doing it but to stay with them. The more we can keep the family united, the more we can help.

LL: Will one of your counsellors visit the home and try to persuade the abuser to stop?

ER: What we do is persuade the child to tell someone. Once the abuser is confronted with the fact that someone else knows what is going on, what the family then most needs is support – but, of course, they can't have it because if the evidence goes to the authorities there is a criminal charge, the man goes to jail, the breadwinner may disappear, the child may end up in care. At the moment, these families have to struggle on without help, and it is terribly difficult for them.

The other thing I would like to say is that sex offenders need tough therapy, they need to understand what they've been doing. They often lie and lie to themselves because frequently they've been abused and cannot handle the knowledge that they are doing to other children what was done to them. Many are sick with self-loathing anyway. If you can break through the carapace of rationalization and excuses, once they can recognize what they've been doing and are offered a way to normality, if you can show them how to hug a child safely and compassionately without sexual feeling – they will take it. Many say they love children, in the genuine sense.

Sending them to jail doesn't help in the long run. Unless they are prepared very clearly to face the fact that they have abused children, that they have caused terrible injury, unless they are prepared to face it and work on it, nothing can be done.

Mary Whitehouse

President of the National Viewers and Listeners'
Association

Mary Whitehouse is a member of my small contemporary pantheon. Emerging as a middle-aged schoolmistress in the early 1960s, she launched and has ever since sustained a campaign against pornography which has reached far beyond these shores. For many years, though things have changed recently, she was howled at but never subdued by student audiences. Whatever one may think about the ubiquity of pornography, things would have been very much worse without her – and as one who chaired a widely publicized committee on pornography in 1971 and 1972, I am in a good position to judge. In the struggle against what I once called a national diet of filth there has been no one to compare with her. It is no surprise to learn that her National Viewers' and Listeners' Association now has 165,000 members.

Four years ago, Mary suffered a serious injury to her back but when I called on her to record the following interview the eyes behind the glasses were as bright as ever, as were her vitality and her passionate belief in the cause.

LORD LONGFORD: I often think about all you have done in the last 30 years in the battle against pornography. In a letter to *The Times*, you called on the public to realize that when a young man does something horrible he may be acting under the influence of very evil media.

MARY WHITEHOUSE: This particular case concerned a 13-year-old boy who had attacked a 14-year-old boy. He had burnt and beaten him and it was an appalling story. The judge said that because he was under age, he could not be imprisoned. I made the point in my

178

letter that it is no good us older people pointing the finger at youngsters and being shocked by what they do because we have normalized so much behaviour which at one time would have been totally unacceptable. We have normalized it through television, through films. Some of the films which are now available and shown are beyond belief.

LL: You mean in cinemas?

MW: Yes, but not only so. Channel 4 has shown films which have not had a certificate.

LL: Is that legal or illegal?

MW: It would perhaps be illegal if they were shown in the cinema, but television is a different matter. That brings us on to the very heart of the problem which increases rather than decreases as time goes by. I refer to the ineffectiveness of the present Obscene Publications Act.

LL: What in your view is the crucial weakness?

MW: We fought for 27 years to get broadcasting brought under the Obscene Publications Act from which it had previously been exempt. We won that battle – at any rate on paper. But because the law is so ineffective – Lord Denning and all sorts of people have said how ineffective it is – it does not do any good for television.

LL: What is the present position about the law in relation to television?

MW: Broadcasting has now been brought under the OPA, which I am very pleased about, but as the law is not any good a tremendous amount of our energy is going into the battle to get the OPA made more effective.

LL: You mean actually altering the law?

MW: Yes, Judge Alan King-Hamilton has prepared an amendment to the OPA which has been offered to the Home Office.

LL: Is the Prime Minister sympathetic?

MW: He always writes personally, and he does say how much he shares our concern.

LL: What is your proposed Bill?

MW: It is a very simple Bill which sets out the aspects of sexual behaviour and pornography which would be considered actionable and hopefully illegal.

LL: What about violence?

MW: Violence comes into it, of course. So far as pornography is concerned, violence is part and parcel of it.

LL: Do you have any special concern about the effect on young people of pornography?

MW: Yes, of course. One of the most fundamental aspects of the effect upon children is that pornography tells them that women and some men are there to be exploited, and often cruelly exploited, that sex is there as an ugly, often violent and obscene aspect of human life. It is feeding into the mind of the child that sex is something ugly, shameful, evil, violent. But sex is not that at all. Pornography destroys the whole of the concept of what human life is about.

LL: But how does that work out?

MW: It undermines, if not destroys, the whole concept of what human life is about. I think when youngsters get hold of this type of material – as inevitably they do – it leads not just to a general disintegration in their thinking but to a very personal disintegration – so that is what Dad does to Mum! These days are meant to be so free and liberated but in fact it is just the reverse.

LL: I wonder how the Feminist movement comes into all this? Are they more against pornography?

MW: They vary, don't they? Some of them care about it from the moral point of view.

LL: You would call yourself a Feminist, wouldn't you?

MW: I never have. My deepest passion and concern is for children. I am concerned about women being used in pornography, of course I am, but I am not driven by Feminist motivation so much as a passion to try to protect the young. That is what it all grew out of.

LL: It is true that you believe in sex education of the right kind?

MW: When I took on a job in 1962 as a senior mistress 'responsible for the moral welfare of the girls', the Newsome Report on the future of secondary education was published a year later. It had a section on sex education which said – and this was the obligation laid upon me as a teacher – that whatever my own feelings may have been, 'sex education must be given on the basis of chastity before marriage and fidelity within it'. Newsome was the most prestigious and forward-looking report we had so far had.

Our school was one of four in the West Midlands that was asked to do some pioneering work in this field. The thing that I discovered quickly was how important it was to involve the parents. After a sex-education class, I always issued questionnaires. In answer to the question, 'Have you discussed the lesson with your parents?', one boy replied, 'Now that I have seen the film I don't feel that I need to talk to my parents.' Instead of helping I felt that we had hindered, so we decided to scrap this approach and start again by inviting the parents to the school.

LL: What did you actually do?

MW: We showed them the film, talked to them and let them choose whether or not their children should be involved in the lessons. We invited mothers and daughters to come together, and fathers and sons. All that work, which was very visionary, got swept away in the flood of the permissive society, but the ideas we pioneered 30 years ago are now beginning to be seen as right and the best way of doing things. You see, it is terribly important that parents know what their children have been told.

LL: Do you think it is the Minister of Education or more the Home Office who ought to be doing something today?

MW: I certainly think that the Minister of Education should look into what is happening. We come back to the impact on the child. When, as I was saying, we had shown a film to the parents, one of them came to me and said, 'Miss, I want to talk to my daughter but I don't know the words to use.' I told her to come to our school and we would teach her the words to use. That was the origin of the work we did with the parents.

LL: How does one teach children about AIDS?

MW: The whole thing has got almost out of control. The argument is that, yes, well, there is a danger of AIDS, so the sooner you tell children and get them to make sure they use condoms, the better. I think that's almost the ultimate indictment of the kind of world we have built – the only thing you can offer needy youngsters is a condom! It challenges the whole quality of our society, the whole quality of our family life.

Another thing that troubles me is the silence of the Church in all of this. The Archbishop of Canterbury has not yet, so far as I know, given any firm guidance to the nation on these issues. The word AIDS and what it involves frightens them all to death. They have grown up in Christian schools and homes where things like this have

181

never permeated. Somebody – and why should it be us? – should be giving leadership in this field.

LL: You have fought against pornography for 30 years. Do you think you have made any difference? Are there any signs of hope?

MW: Yes – what gives me so much hope is that the attitude of the young has changed. Right from the beginning of our campaign, I have spoken in universities up and down the country and across the world – and I have had everything thrown at me both verbally and physically. But they now sit and listen, and I win my debates. I have not changed – it is the young who have changed. The heart of the young is good and right, and I believe that the people who have to change are the older generation.

There are three pieces of legislation on the statute book now that sprang primarily from our work – the Indecent Displays Act, the Child Protection Act, and the Video Recordings Act. Then there is the work we are doing to tighten up the Obscene Publications Act. We fought a long battle to remove the clause that excluded broadcasting from the Act, and that happened in November 1991.

LL: So your priority is to get the Obscene Publications Act made more effective?

MW: There is no question about it. I know that the New Scotland Yard Obscene Publications Department are very pleased that efforts for new legislation of this kind are being made, because they are now powerless.

LL: Do you feel that schools could be encouraged to improve sex education?

MW: There is probably quite a lot of reasonable sex education being given in schools, but there are pressures all the time, particularly over AIDS, and there are those who think we should start sex education at 5, 6, 7 years old. I find myself flatly against that because it destroys the children's childhood. That's one of the worst aspects of it. The magic, the dream, the wonder of childhood – it's all being destroyed by the pressures on the child to be adult. What hope is there for the individual child or for society? 'Better a millstone be hung around your neck than that one of my little ones should suffer.' I think that some of us could do with a bit of millstone round our neck.

LL: How should young offenders be treated? The general view is that they should not be sent to prison but that some sort of constructive regime should be provided.

MW: I am not sure that sending youngsters to prison does anything for them. I do not know what the alternative really is – what kind of care. Their parents also need help at the same time.

LL: All these things come back to the moral state of the nation. Do you feel that Church leaders should be giving a lead?

MW: Absolutely. Let's look into ourselves. I always remember a woman who came up to me and said, 'Mrs Whitehouse, I am so grateful for everything you do.' I said, 'Don't be grateful to me. The real question is, What are you doing?' That's the point of view all of us need to build on.

John Mortimer

President of the Howard League for Penal Reform

John Mortimer is equally well known as an eminent QC and as a very popular writer on everything to do with the law. He is an accomplished playwright and novelist, he is the creator of Rumpole of the Bailey, and recently he edited *The Oxford Book of Villains*. John Mortimer is an all-round liberal humanitarian.

LORD LONGFORD: Has your long practical experience of law given you any special approach to offenders?

JOHN MORTIMER: I began with my legal career. For about the first 15 years, I followed my father who specialized in probate and wills; I did that area until I took silk. I 'took to crime' late in life. I actually found clients in criminal cases rather nicer. Human nature is at its worst in a probate action for grandmother's furniture. When I did crime I did quite a specialized form, defending many dubious books, which is hardly a crime in that sense, versus Mary Whitehouse; I have tremendous respect for her courage. I kept to the sort of crime which was not hard bank robbery and professional crime but murders where ordinary people killed somebody.

LL: In your anthology of villains there is a lot of murder—

JM: Yes, but by ordinary people. I always defended, never prosecuted except once, when some railway policemen had been chaining ticket collectors to railings and generally behaving badly. Unfortunately my instincts as defender were too strong, and the police got off!

My attitude to offenders is a defender's attitude – never sit in judgement, that's for the judge. They were people who had chosen me to defend them, which immediately puts me on their side. Many

184

tend to blot out of their minds the horrific things they've done.

LL: Is it a condition of mental survival?

JM: Yes, they might have killed the person bullying them. Afterwards they become strangely peaceful – and very grateful for what you do for them.

LL: Because they have been under some tension that has been released?

JM: Yes. Murders go on between families, mothers and sons, husbands and wives, a long close relationship. If it gets too close, the act of killing that person does create peace of mind. They're very grateful, and cause no trouble after that.

I've always thought of the law as a kind of disease, with me as the doctor; that the law is like a sickness, and I had to bring patients through as painlessly as possible. A lot is attributable to poverty and unemployment, boredom, no direction in life – life today doesn't offer idealism, there's been a draining recently, there's nothing to believe in. A young unemployed person on the street, stealing a car for a joy-ride, beats boredom. But if they catch you, you get sent to prison and learn to be a real professional.

LL: You know Jimmy Boyle and speak well of him?

JM: Jimmy Boyle was a man convicted of murder in Scotland. He was a total rebel, so bad that the authorities ended up putting him naked in a cage. He was transferred to the Barlinnie Special Unit, and wrote a play. He is now totally reformed and runs a drug unit.

Jimmy Boyle once said that if you were brought up in the Gorbals, crime was the thing to do. I don't believe that's true – many people from comfortable homes are criminals. What people don't realize is the excitement – it's like skiing or hunting, when you're at risk. There is a most revealing story told by a bank robber to Laurie Taylor. He felt that crime is this great secret you have – like Batman, everyone reads of what you've done, but only you know it's you. Evil can be exciting.

LL: Are there people who are essentially evil?

JM: There is a spirit of evil abroad, an abstract thing, and it has its part in Nazi rallies, the Klu Klux Klan. If you want to combat crime you must combat social deprivation. You must make the good life more exciting than the criminal life.

LL: What about the prison system?

JM: There are incredibly good and dedicated people among prison warders but the system can overwhelm them. A survey was taken asking if they wanted to be seen as police or probation officers – the majority said probation officers.

People have to be offered alternative excitement in their lives. Our lives are exciting, so we don't need the excitement of crime. Take Rumpole, came from a legal family, went into law – my father was a barrister, I am. You are an Earl, so was your father. If you come from a criminal family, crime is your profession.

LL: But children from good families go to bad too?

JM: That's true, they want to be different, to rebel. When I started in crime there were four courts; now there are 30. Only 5 per cent of crime is violent crime, not that you'd think it by reading the newspapers. In fact the people at greatest risk are young men aged 16–21, from other young men. It's nothing to say that we have a lower murder rate than America, but ours is also lower than Canada or Australia.

LL: Yet the crime rate continually increases?

JM: Papers want to make society look as lurid as possible. We all have basic instincts – the standard defence of pornography cases is that it's better to read about it than do it. But Britain is the most penal-minded country; we have more prisoners per head of population than Turkey.

LL: If you were in a position to do something, what would it be?

JM: Cut the prison population by one-third. The Germans found they lowered the crime rate by doing that.

The very first reform should be to make every judge serve an indefinite sentence in prison, not necessarily long, but unsure of when he'll get out! Judges have no experience of prison life. They have no idea what they're sending people to. A few nights in the cells would help. We have people in prison for not paying their TV licence or alimony, for not paying the poll tax. You could halve the numbers in prison.

LL: Have you had any contact with senior ministers?

JM: As President of the Howard League, yes. I visited Mr Patten, then Minister for Prisons, and Mr Baker, then Home Secretary, about so many 15-year-olds committing suicide in custody, mainly on remand. Girls are not put in prison on remand – it's very sexist. We got a good reception but Mr Baker said, 'You must go on protesting. We are horrified here. Unfortunately sentencing is a matter for the judges and they can't be controlled by us. We may have some solution in four years' time. And we have no money. Local authorities have no money either.'

LL: Would you agree that no one should go to custody under the age of 18?

JM: Yes, though some may need to be under restraint, but it should not be in adult prisons. The government solution is to build more prisons. No judge or anyone I've met thought prison actually did any good. The defence of prison is that it keeps them out of circulation. It depends on the crime as to whether it is a deterrent. Criminals have insane optimism; especially in fraud cases, they sincerely believe the day of reckoning will never come. When there was the death penalty for stealing hankies, hankies still got stolen.

In Germany, you start life as a judge very young, around 23. German judges are now the product of the Flower Power generation, whereas ours are very elderly.

LL: What about the search for self-esteem among criminals?

JM: I think they're cocky and pleased with themselves until they're caught – the professional ones, that is. But others stumble into crime.

When I used to see them on trial they occupied a starring role. The Old Bailey is a great place for jokes; many were on a high. That is also what's bad about young people getting a Great Day in Court, having attention paid to them. Without them, judges would be out of a job.

LL: What is the alternative to prison?

JM: The condition of prisons is a total disgrace. They are a breeding place for crime. The deterrent effect is far less than the criminal education it produces. Quintin Hogg used to say that he agreed but that the punishment is being deprived of liberty. That must be remedied by a drastic reduction in the prison population. There should be secure, decent places for those who have to be removed from society.

LL: What about the victims?

JM: The victims of crime are much more interested in compensation than retribution. Criminals should work to compensate them. But the legal profession and prison administrators are star-struck about criminals. Solicitors show off and call famous criminals by their first names. In the mid-70s, there was a case where the butler and the footman of a Labour MP murdered him. It turned out that the butler had done many murders. He buried the victims in Scotland when he found out that a Not Proven verdict was applicable there. After they were caught and locked up, the footman said that the butler was treated like a star for all the murders he'd done, but the footman, with only a few, was ignored.

LL: Mary Whitehouse is sure that pornography causes crime and corruption, especially among the young. How do you feel?

JM: Nothing has ever been proved. The young aren't interested, they do it for real, they don't need to read about it. Pornography is mostly for middle-aged men! There was no pornography, or at least very little, in the eighteenth century when there was a lot of crime. I never read it because I could defend it more effectively without knowing about it. It is an impossible thing to legislate on; the dangers of censorship are greater than the dangers of pornography. All freedom carries great risks.

Edward Fitzgerald
Barrister at Law

Edward Fitzgerald is a barrister who practises at the Criminal Bar and who is married to my eldest granddaughter. He has made a great reputation already as a champion of prisoners' rights.

LORD LONGFORD: Edward: you have had experience of young offenders both in an approved school and over a number of years at the Criminal Bar. Could you say a word or two about your experience in an approved school? Could you tell me whether you formed any idea *then* about young offenders, and whether you have developed them since?

EDWARD FITZGERALD: When I was working at Kingswood Training School in 1977 I believed, as most of the workers did, very much in the possibilities of treating children by taking them away from the home environment.

LL: Can you give me a word or two about this place?

EF: The inmates were aged from 10 to 19 years, most of them between 12 and 17. There were 50 in the assessment centre, 60 in the training school and 20 in the special secure unit.

LL: Can you give me a few words about the special unit?

EF: I was just a volunteer. Staff? Some were fully qualified social workers, some had experience in child care and some no training at all. They were a mixed, committed staff, with a tremendous belief in what they were doing. This was a time when the philosophy of therapy and of the notion of a therapeutic community was being jettisoned for the more punitive approach. The idea was self-govern-

189

ment by the boys. The general view was that that was not working. There was a return to a more paternalistic and perhaps retributive approach.

LL: Did you have psychiatrists and psychologists?

EF: Yes, but there was no individual therapy. There were group meetings. It was believed that community experience should provide therapy.

LL: You were satisfied with the ethos?

EF: I believed that it was good to take children away from homes where they were exposed to psychological stresses and put them into a community where more care and love could be provided. That was the purpose. Thinking back, I am critical. In many cases it did harm. If you think you are doing good to people, you build up a philosophy where magistrates are more prepared to send children away from home and social workers recommend it. Most of the boys resented being sent away from home intensely, however. They saw it as punishment, whatever they were told about it being treatment. Most of them had been convicted of offences.

LL: What proportion?

EF: Some 85 per cent convicted. Some had been persistent absconders and out of control.

LL: To what extent did the young people consider their punishment to be disproportionate?

EF: The career plan tended to be that they should stay there for nine months to two years. That was far longer than was merited by their offences. In the name of therapy, their normal existence was taken away. Most of the pupils would have preferred a short, sharp treatment. The punishment was disproportionate to the offence.

LL: Should young people be treated more leniently than adults?

EF: Yes, partly because the reasons for their offending tend, in great measure, not to be of their own making. They are less free agents. Again, the punishment of being deprived of your liberty is felt more harshly when young – it is wasting the most valuable years of your life. If they commit serious crimes, they should be punished. The punishment should have a ceiling, determined on grounds of proportionality. We should not delude ourselves with the idea that young people should serve longer periods, in order to get better treatment. On the whole, one could punish them in the community.

190

LL: Community? Recently three boys of 15 were found guilty of raping a girl of 13. What do you do with them?

EF: It is not wrong to sentence them to a period of custody, in my view. I suspect that one has to accept that custody will be pretty similar for juveniles wherever it is, but don't let us have imprisonment in adult institutions. Care provided by social workers is my preference. The institution has got to be based on the needs of young children. Loss of liberty is always punishment. But within that framework, we must have a clear concept that they are to be helped and improved while in custody. I am not advocating a soft approach so much as an effective one. It will always be penal if you take liberty away. In the context of punitive custody, you must have education.

LL: We must try to keep them out of custody.

EF: It is essential to try to devise community punishments – living at home and putting more resources into supervision. We need rigorous punishment in the community, with a custodial long-stop for those who do not carry out the orders given.

LL: What about young thugs?

EF: Young thugs who burgle an old lady should be made to pay back in an obvious way. An element of punishment and indignity is not inappropriate. The problem is the will of the Probation Service who are going to implement the schemes. Some probation officers feel that it is not their role to dish out punishment. Community service should be expiation. If it is not made that way, then magistrates and judges will feel that the only way they can meet criminal behaviour is by custody.

LL: Any additional thoughts?

EF: Two reforms immediately suggest themselves in connection with lifer's rights. All enlightened people agree that the mandatory life sentence should be abolished. Life sentences for people under 18 should be got rid of at once. The use of an indeterminate sentence for lesser offences should be controlled for those under 18. The moment they reach 18, a review before a court should be required. The court should have the power to disapply any indeterminate sentence imposed.

LL: Anything else?

EF: The areas which require special attention are obviously those which involve the imprisonment of anyone under 17. That should be outlawed forthwith.

Paul Boateng

Member of Parliament for Brent South

Paul Boateng was called to the Bar in 1989, having originally qualified as a solicitor. He was a leading member of the Greater London Council from 1981 to 1986, during which time he was also on the Police Training Council, and he has been a Governor of the Police Staff College at Bramshill. Mr Boateng has been Labour MP for Brent South since 1987.

LORD LONGFORD: Would you say that black people are treated worse than whites in the UK when suspected of breaking the law?

PAUL BOATENG: All the evidence is that there is still a tendency to stereotype people in the criminal system – at all levels. Black youngsters are more likely to be suspected and they are less likely just to be cautioned; more likely to have a custodial sentence if convicted. Yes, there are still patterns of discrimination despite undoubted efforts to improve, particularly since the urban uprisings in the early '80s.

LL: Do you think that the Scarman Inquiry achieved something?

PB: On reflection, that period brought society face to face with what was happening. Many areas were seen to be policed by an occupying force – the police were seen as brutal and communities felt alienated. This was not exclusive to black youngsters. If you look back, and even more in the case of recent disturbances, many white youngsters have been involved. Some have even been exclusively white, as in Oxford.

LL: Do you think it is a vicious circle, where communities are hostile to police, so the police are hostile back?

PB: There is a real degree of mutual suspicion between black people and the police which inevitably manifests itself in confrontational situations. It is more likely if a police officer sees a young black in a middle-class setting. For example, I did a case for a very middle-class family, one of whose children was stopped on a leafy suburban road in Putney Hill. The officer is alleged to have said, 'What's someone like you doing in a place like this? You must be here to sus for burglary.' The lad actually lived there! This type of attitude obviously leads to bitterness. It is important to understand that there are parts of London where Afro-Caribbean youngsters gather on street corners, outside a club, in the open air, because that's the cultural pattern, and yes, they do have ghetto-blasters. They are likely to be talking in street language which the police may not understand.

LL: They speak a type of patois?

PB: Not original patois – many of them have never been to the Caribbean in their lives. Black street language has been adopted by whites. One of the interesting phenomena in youth culture is the way black rap impacts on youth black and white – fashion, culture, speech and music. It's not a situation where black and white youth are totally separate. That has passed, except that stereotyping and grievance among black youth remain.

LL: Are black youngsters more likely to come from a broken home?

PB: They are more likely to come from a single-parent home. Many youngsters have never had a father-figure; the mother is the only source of stability. I'm not West Indian – I am of African and Scottish origin – but I know there are very strong family links in Barbados, for example. Increasingly, certainly in my constituency, more children are born to single mothers across the board, black and white. I'm not convinced about the link between single mothers and offending.

LL: But it is not a good start. Can they get on from there? What about the Bar?

PB: It is getting better. When I began I was often the only black, but now you can go to Magistrates' and Crown Courts, and there will be a black judge, defence counsel, court usher, and the defendant is white!

LL: How far have blacks got on the promotional ladder?

PB: Not far enough – there are no black High Court judges, three or four black full-time Crown Court judges, about eight Recorders and Assistant Recorders, so there is a long way to go. It is worse for women.

LL: What tends to happen to black youngsters on conviction?

PB: My experience of penal institutions is that they are appalling – they are brutalizing and don't give sufficient attention to training and education. The remand situation is even worse, and overall these places are breeding grounds for crime and despair. That applies to both black and white. It is very important to remember when you are recruiting for officers, welfare workers and so on in such institutions that black offenders need positive role models to help rehabilitation. Black prison or probation officers need to be particularly sensitive.

LL: Do you think the white officers are often racist?

PB: Black police officers have a tough time. I'm not so sure that is the case for prison officers, but there is a need to encourage black people to become prison officers and there's a need for better rewards for those tasks.

It is no use just to wish there were more black police officers or believe either that the simple adoption of equal opportunities policies will ensure that. There need to be positive policies. Becoming a policeman is not the automatic choice for immigrants. After all, it's a thankless, difficult task. They want their kids to be teachers or nurses. For example, how many Jewish police officers are there?

LL: What is the remedy, then?

PB: Look at the USA. It is not the number of ethnic minorities in the force that matters, but their ability to influence the force. In the States, black youngsters have an opportunity to progress in the police, fire service, politics, the army. They need good and positive role models. It's never been a solution just to have more black officers *per se*.

LL: Do blacks think it is being Uncle Tom to join?

PB: It is regarded as a bizarre and masochistic option as a career. At first they have a hard time and get hassle from some of their more ignorant colleagues. I have certainly met black officers that find the canteen culture offensive – just as women find it offensive. But it is important to recognize that considerable steps have been made in the past 10–12 years by the police under pressure from the community and judiciary – Scarman, civil liberties groups, all have had an impact. But we can't afford to be complacent – racism is still an issue.

194

LL: So we must look at the wider causes. Blacks are more likely to be unemployed, for example?

PB: Yes, they are also likely to be disadvantaged.

LL: Would positive discrimination help?

PB: In employment law and race relations, we should have effective equal opportunity legislation. We need to monitor employment practices in both the private and public sectors to ensure fair deals and remedy the appalling state of schools for both black and white. Educational disadvantage is not just confined to black youngsters – there can't be a simplistic approach. But there is alienation, because the system is not delivering fair shares.

There also needs to be a focus on the judiciary – there is a huge under-resource of alternatives to custody. We must look at the tendency of judges not to use alternatives to custody for blacks. The Home Office's own statistics show this, which is why the Lord Chancellor is so concerned to increase race relation training for the judiciary.

LL: No judge would admit it.

PB: It is institutional, indirect racism, subconscious; a tendency to assume that black youngsters have a greater propensity to violence, are less likely to be amenable to non-custodial treatment, are more threatening. Significantly, there is still evidence – although this changes with recession – that if you don't have a job or a home, you are more likely to get a custodial sentence.

IV
Young Offenders

I Aycliffe Hospital

'You can't write a book on young offenders without going to Aycliffe' – so spoke Lucy Faithfull, my admired friend and expert on all social matters, especially where young people are concerned. Others said the same. So on Friday 31 July 1992, I duly reported at Aycliffe, which is near Darlington.

Soon I was involved in very profitable discussions with the Deputy Director and the Head of Children's Services. A good many of the things they told me can be summarized as follows:

Aycliffe is a specialized facility for young people who present or experience serious difficulties. Typically, they have a long history of disordered behaviour and have failed to respond to previous attempts at helping them, often by other specialists. The young people come from the whole of the UK, because those responsible for them believe that, notwithstanding distance, the Aycliffe service is better than they get elsewhere. However, we are probably even more effective with younger and less seriously damaged youngsters who would benefit from a shorter period of focused work at Aycliffe, to be supported in the home area when they have left.

Most of the young people come from unstable and disordered family backgrounds. However emotionally attached the families may be, in real terms they find it difficult to give their children adequate and appropriate care and control. Because of this and the impact of other people's intervention in their lives, the young people believe themselves to be unlovable and unworthy of care. They therefore find it difficult to care for themselves or other people. They often behave as if they bear a deep grievance, are beyond control and have no real hope for their future. Because of this, they 'let rip', cause havoc and seek further to fulfil the prophecy that no one genuinely cares for them or is prepared to persevere with them through the thick and thin of difficult adolescence.

Most of the young people at Aycliffe are between 14 and 18 years

199

old, though some are younger and some are older. It is well staffed quantitatively and qualitatively. The full complement of children is 122, with a staff of 200 professionals and up to 100 others. A ratio of 2 staff to 1 young person is a fair way of looking at it. The previous day I had visited Albatross, the therapeutic unit at Feltham. There, 8 staff have to cope with 20 inmates.

Sixty-five to seventy per cent of the staff possess formal qualifications. The rest possess qualifications of some kind – one young woman has a first class degree in Classics. The professional staff are a mix of educationalists, social workers, psychologists and nurses. It should be understood that Aycliffe prides itself on being an educational establishment. The point is worth labouring. It is often assumed that if young offenders are not sent to penal custody they are sent instead to some kind of hospital, a local authority secure unit or to some form of intermediate treatment or probation set-up.

Aycliffe's Director, I gathered, is a psychologist, but both the Deputy Director and the Head of Children's Services are professional educationalists with some psychological training. Despite their high ideals and numerical strength, I have the impression that the staff labour under considerable strain. A senior member was bitten three times by a boy who was at Feltham from the age of 11 to 16. The same boy bit other members of staff. It is not surprising that there is a considerable turnover of staff at Aycliffe, but I was reminded that in many comparable institutions the turnover is more like 40 per cent each year.

The cost of keeping a young person in Aycliffe is admittedly high – £75,000 a year for those in secure conditions (about 50 out of 122) and £50,000 for the rest. This compares with £100,000 a year at St Charles, and much less for care in the community. There is no shirking the fact that adequate care for these disturbed youngsters is very expensive by any normal standard.

I visited the secure wing. It was a very hot day and I was glad that I was not confined there, although the youngsters spend some hours outside – a great improvement on many penal institutions where inmates can be locked up for 23 hours a day. So far as I could judge the young people were reasonably happy. One showed me with pride three rooms he had painted including his own. He was small and gentle, with a soft handshake. It was difficult to believe that he had been one of the ringleaders in a riot.

Aycliffe is profoundly impressive, and visitors come from all over the world to study its methods. The psychological approach is behaviouristic. To put it crudely, someone who arrives with bad antisocial habits is helped to overcome them by practical activities.

However, I was a little disappointed at the reply to my question, Why shouldn't we replicate Aycliffe? – as at present the children have to come from all over the country, and many of us have asked the same question for years about Grendon psychiatric prison. But the Deputy Director and the Head of Children's Services pointed out to me that Rome wasn't built in a day: it had taken 50 years to create the present Aycliffe, and another could not be started overnight. Even so, I could not see why a beginning should not be made. What is the point of a centre of excellence if it is not imitated?

Be that as it may, it was a very inspiring visit.

II Fairbridge

There is such a wealth of enlightened attempts to provide alternatives to penal custody that it is somewhat invidious to pick out one project rather than another. But it would be impossible to avoid making reference to Fairbridge. Originally, the Fairbridge Society (as the secular charity was called when founded in 1909) aimed to educate abandoned British children in farm schools in Canada and Australia. Today, Fairbridge operates from 13 inner-city bases in Britain, and uses its annual budget of around £2 million to provide outdoor motivational training with the aim of harnessing young people's imagination and energy, particularly those whom one might call the victims of inner-city life.

John Huskins, Her Majesty's Inspector for the Department of Education and Science, referred to Fairbridge in his report for April to July 1990. Under the heading 'Adventure Experiences for Young People from Urban Areas', he said: 'If you want an example of good practice within the inner cities you need look no further than Fairbridge.'

In their 1991 Annual Review, Fairbridge identified their 'Three Great Strengths'. Let me paraphrase:

1. Fairbridge is closely focused on young people at risk.

2. It has highly trained and professional staff with a great knowledge of the problems and needs of young people, and a remarkable ability to establish effective relationships with them.

3. It works. Fairbridge passionately believes that young people have unlimited potential and is incredibly successful at releasing it. In addition, Fairbridge is committed to staff training to achieve greater quality, safety and excellence. With understandable pride, they

202

announce that all this has made a huge difference to the 15,016 young people they worked with in 1991. These 15,016 were spread over 13 units. With equally justified pride, the Annual Review informs us that six out of ten people who went on the basic motivation or training course went on to get jobs, took up or returned to training or education, or secured voluntary work in the community.

I visited the Fairbridge headquarters and one of their units. At the headquarters I had a helpful talk with a young man who had been in prison, went on to receive training at Fairbridge and was now on the staff. About 30 per cent of the staff, I gather, have been in trouble with the law. The proportion of ex-offenders who attend the various centres would seem to vary a good deal. To take one example from Mr Huskins' report: 'In Bristol there has been a gradual shift towards recruiting young offenders who now comprise almost half the intake – 29 per cent of participants coming from probation hostels and a further 17 per cent being referred by the Probation Service. These young people display a variety of behavioural difficulties and problems and present a considerable challenge to the staff to motivate them and to develop their potential.' There are, indeed, two distinctive feature of Fairbridge, apart from a dedication widely shared elsewhere. To quote Mr Huskins again: 'Local authority youth services and voluntary youth organizations offer a rich variety of adventure activities designed to motivate and provide learning experience for disadvantaged adolescents from urban areas. ... Youth workers relate well to these young people, display sensitivity and skills in group work, and manage the courses efficiently. The most successful projects have close links with a local community, young people are selected carefully, and are provided with long-term support and encouragement.'

The other distinctive feature is summed up in the phrase already quoted from the Inspector's report: 'Adventure Experiences for Young People from Urban Areas'. Fairbridge developed the idea of making available residential experience at adventure centres in the West Highlands of Scotland and on a sail training ship. Arduous adventure is very much part of the Fairbridge attempt to encourage personal confidence and motivation among those not very likely to possess it. But the lofty purpose brings in its train an inevitable difficulty. As the Inspector says, 'The young people needing the training can be identified in the catchment area but their lack of motivation, which contributes to their employment and behavioural difficulties and frequently leads to offending, makes it difficult for them to overcome their uncertainty about a course which requires a ten-day commitment, five days of which are under canvas, among strangers.' Fairbridge's adventure programmes will never appeal to more than a limited proportion of young people, but Fairbridge itself has provided and continues to provide an inspiration and a means of redemption to thousands.

III St Charles Youth Treatment Centre

The purpose of St Charles, in its own words, is 'to help extremely disturbed boys and girls, aged 13–18, whose special needs cannot be met elsewhere. Complex factors are likely to have impaired social and emotional personal development and control. They may be a danger to themselves, others or both.'

Adults so described would be either in prison, or in a mental hospital, possibly a secure hospital. Until I visited St Charles, which is in Brentwood in Essex, I had not realized that it was intended for such a specialized type of resident. Thirty places are available there at a cost of £100,000 per person per year, with a ratio of 90 staff to 30 patients. It is not likely that treatment on this scale could be multiplied many times, but the treatment surely has lessons of wide application.

For the most part the residents are confined to the premises, but towards the end of their stay they are given the opportunity to work outside. One young man I met is working as a trainee hairdresser. He is only 16, and could have another two years at St Charles.

The regime includes a great deal of education, and I was amused to be told that attendance at these classes is compulsory – but 'participation' is not! I understand that most of the young people 'participate' in practice.

St Charles's residential population is mixed, although the ratio of boys to girls is 6 to 1. The average age of admission is just over 16, with disturbed youngsters on average a year older. The residents that I met could fairly be described as having been and perhaps still were extremely disturbed, although young people who are mentally ill are not admitted.

During my visit I met two arsonists and a rather undersized boy who was said to have been violent at school. While at St Charles he had tried to strangle a lady educationalist by grabbing her from behind and tying a shoe-lace round her neck. When I asked him to explain his conduct, he could only tell me: 'We did not like her.' I surmised that he was trying to impress a gang who might otherwise have despised him.

The Director had no doubt that St Charles was doing a useful job in keeping these young people out of the penal system. One asks oneself the obvious question: What is the difference between this kind of custody and penal custody, apart from the much higher staff ratio and the stigma attaching to any sort of imprisonment? One obvious difference is that the staff at St Charles are a mixture of trained teachers, nurses and probation officers, much more qualified therefore as 'carers' than prison officers could be. Senior clinical psychologists, leaving-care co-ordinators, consultant psychiatrists and studies staff also contribute to the St Charles regime.

The Dartington Social Research Unit, to which I have referred, conducted a very thorough inquiry into the subsequent lives of young men leaving St Charles. Their finding, in summary, is that centres like St Charles do help young people to come to terms with their families and they do provide former residents with considerable support as they settle in the outside world – in contrast to the often minimal support provided through the penal system. It is not surprising, however, that 'boys that have been long in care or custody and whose family links have withered present depressing careers on leaving'. In this regard Dartington stress the need for improvements in aftercare, but conclude that 'There is little indication that better aftercare will dramatically affect the offending of young people'.

The Dartington report fluctuates between good news and bad. On the one hand, 'The living situations and family relationships of centre-leavers offer encouragement' – but on the other side, 'Offending is one aspect of these young people's general conduct disorders which seems to remain intractable'. On balance, however, St Charles is a ray of hope, and the great majority of its young people secure lasting benefits from their treatment. Penal reformers can only applaud Dartington's conclusions: 'By definition the entrants to the centres are among the most difficult children in the country. ... The difficulty of this work is to find staff capable of working well in the context of endless defeat and failure, but if such staff can be found – and many childcare establishments along with the centres enjoy the devotion of such people – then surely it is obligatory on local authorities to offer treatment settings, support and encouragement.'

IV The Probation Service

It would be impossible even to begin to describe the many projects of the Probation Service which go far beyond its traditional role of friendly supervision. I will refer to a couple that I have visited myself. On 15 April 1992, I visited the Stevenage Probation Day Centre. The Chief Officer and his team left me in no doubt about the value of their work. To quote from one of their reports:

A Home Office inspection led to the allocation of extra funds to provide the purpose-built Probation Centres and the staff for them. The Probation Centre at Stevenage College opened in January 1989 and was followed by the Dacorum Centre in November the same year. The programme offered at both centres is called the New Opportunity Programme. It is a joint venture with the Hertfordshire Education Authority, hence the siting of the Centres in Colleges of Further Education.

Over the last two and a half years, I was told, more than 100 clients had joined the New Opportunity Programme. More than two-thirds of these had left secondary education with no examinations taken or passed. Indeed, more than half of them had left school early in their final year or before that. Approximately a quarter of all clients had been taken out of mainstream schooling to attend a variety of special education settings – from special units to boarding schools. The staff includes two senior tutors – one of them said to me that despite their previous educational failure, he did not regard his pupils as mentally subnormal.

I told the Chief Probation Officer that I was so impressed with what I had seen that I wondered whether the Stevenage Centre was not to be multiplied. Rather to my surprise, he firmly disagreed. He felt that more centres of this kind might lead to a number of petty offenders being brought under unnecessary supervision, and that the more serious offenders might find the regime too uncomfortable for them to keep the rules. They would therefore finish in prison with a further blot on their record. This brought out the point that the regime at Stevenage is by no means an easy option. The attendance several times a week involves a one-hour's journey both ways for many clients – leaving some of them, I was told, claiming that prison would be a softer option.

I next visited the Leeds Probation Service. They are engaged in all sorts of far-sighted initiatives, but I was most interested in their Young Adult Offenders Project for 1990–1. I was told that the project is based on eight fundamental principles, of which two in particular held my attention.

First, the project accepts the fundamentally negative aspect of custody upon the individual which further compounds offending behaviour and attitudes.

In the second place, the project is based on the belief that a caring and structured approach which concentrates on the specific needs of the individual is the best way forward in dealing with young adult offenders. Perhaps the simplest way of illustrating the approach in practice is from one of their cases. David, aged 18 years, is serving a sentence for four offences of theft and three of burglary. He has been offending since the age of 14. In his first week on the project, the task is one of action. He meets the probation officer, his circumstances are reviewed, and a visit is arranged to a drug agency. In the second week he is helped to develop ability and to exercise self-control, and these skills are built on for the next six weeks. In the eighth week, the probation officer and his project worker meet to discuss a programme and to plan for the remainder of David's probation order. They key factor, however, is that David is seen by his project worker three times a week – much more often than he would normally be by a probation officer. At the end of the programme, a judicial feedback report is sent to the sentencing judge. David said that the programme was 'good because it learned me how to keep out of trouble. I hope that others get the chance to come on this project. I stayed out of trouble by not doing any offences by thinking first.'

A book on young offenders cannot avoid some reference to intensive probation (IP), although it is not specifically for young offenders. Intensive probation was intended, in the words of the Home Office, to be 'a developmental experimental initiative'. In April 1990, intensive probation schemes were set up in nine areas, with the aim of adding IP programmes to another ten areas before the end of 1991.

Intensive probation has five principal aims.

1. To set up rigorous referral and selection procedures in order that low-risk offenders will not be subjected to IP – that is to say, to confine IP to those who most need it.

2. To work out a comprehensive, personalized programme with the offender and to present this to the court.

3. To focus on confronting offending behaviour.

4. To use a multi-agency approach whereby the skills of both voluntary and statutory agencies are utilized.

5. To include ethnic minority and female offenders in the programmes.

It is still too early to pronounce on the success of IP. Even so, it is quite clear that if it is to work IP will demand the fullest co-operation from the Probation Service and confidence on the part of the courts and the police that it is not a soft option – as is sometimes alleged of probation generally.

Perhaps we should refine the aims of intensive probation as follows:

1. To divert appropriate offenders in the 17–25 age group from penal custody.

2. To demonstrate that offenders can be safely supervised in the programme, and that the reconviction rates at two years after sentence compare favourably to those of similar offenders who have served sentences of imprisonment.

3. To demonstrate that IP can have a positive impact on the personal circumstances of offenders who complete the programme.

4. To demonstrate that the approach can be cost-effective.

No doubt when IP is fully off the ground, attempts will be made to measure its achievements. In the meantime, I return to the Leeds Young Adult Offenders Project, where I feel sure that I can report a success story. From all that I saw and heard during my visit, there have been many such Davids.

V Intermediate Treatment

Mr D. W. Jones, the Assistant Director of the Intermediate Treatment Fund, was kind enough to explain to me the story of intermediate treatment from the inside. I will only quote one passage from his evidence regarding what the Fund actually does:

1. It gives grants. Social workers and probation officers refer people for supervision.

2. It gives advice and assistance to projects (voluntary groups) that it supports.

3. It attracts funding from other charities. For every £1 that it receives from the State, it receives £5 from other charities.

4. It is seen by the government as an advice and pressure agency, helping the voluntary sector.

The evidence already given to me by Lord Hunt (see page 167) brings out two of the most essential points:

1. Intermediate treatment is by no means directed mainly to these who have been convicted by the court, but predominantly to those at risk. In North Lambeth I was told that only one of the nine intermediate treatment centres (the Junction Project, which I visited) was intended primarily for young offenders.

2. The connection between the treatment and the prevention of crime is of predominant concern.

With the second point in mind, no one interested in the question should refrain from reading *Juvenile Offending* (1989) by Sarah Curtis (see page 59). In particular, its sub-title should be noted: *Prevention through Intermediate Treatment*. I asked Mrs Curtis when

210

I interviewed her whether her book still represented her views. 'Very much so,' she replied. Some 21 of her proposals have since been put into law under the Criminal Justice Act of 1991. Seventeen-year-olds have, from October 1992, been included in the jurisdiction of the Juvenile Court (now the Youth Court). Family Courts, of one of which Mrs Curtis is Chairman, have been introduced. All her summarized proposals in *Juvenile Offending* should be given most careful consideration, in addition to the demand stressed during our interview that much more adequate resources should be made available.

There seems to be general agreement with Mrs Curtis that the term 'intermediate treatment' should be dropped in favour of clearer titles for projects and services. I myself agree whole-heartedly with her recommendations. I am left wondering, however, whether attendance requirements in the centres I have visited have been adequate for the purpose of achieving a new self-esteem and a new approach to society among the young, which all well-intentioned people have in mind.

VI The Children and Young Persons Act, 1933

In June 1991, the Prince's Trust produced a most valuable report on two Sections of the Children and Young Persons Act, 1933. Section 53(1) deals with persons under the age of 18 convicted of murder. Section 53(2) deals with persons under the age of 17 convicted of an offence for which an adult might be sentenced to 14 years' imprisonment or more and for whom no other disposal is considered suitable by the court. Both groups are to be detained during Her Majesty's Pleasure as the Home Secretary may direct. The period of detention, which may be for life, must be specified in the sentence and must not exceed the maximum period of imprisonment with which the offence would be punishable in the case of an adult. The study was most efficiently conducted by Dr Boswell of the University of East Anglia.

In the course of her research, she interviewed 25 young people sentenced under Section 53. Six of those interviewed are described in the report. Three of them were serving quite short sentences – two years for arson, one year for robbery, two and a half years for assault – but three were detained during Her Majesty's Pleasure, two for murder and one for assault causing grievous bodily harm. On the whole, they do not seem to have been very much dissatisfied with their treatment.

It is highly revealing that most but not all of these young people start their sentence in community homes in the child care system, pass to young offender institutions and finish up in adult prisons. Of the 614 young people involved at the time of the inquiry, 135 (aged 10 to 20) were in community homes or youth treatment centres; 267 (aged 15 to 20 – note the inclusion of some 15 and 16-year-olds) were in young offender institutions; and the remain-

212

der, 212 (over 21 years old), were in adult prisons.

Broadly speaking, Dr Boswell passed favourable comments on the arrangements made for these young offenders while in community homes and youth treatment centres. She becomes a good deal more critical when they pass to young offender institutions and very critical indeed when dealing with their lives in adult prisons. She makes a number of concrete recommendations which include:

1. A brief and simply worded manual to help people to continue any work already begun on their offending behaviour.

2. A consultant should be assigned to counsel and inform members of the offender group at key stages in their sentence.

3. Much more adequate information about education should be made available to offenders.

4. The production of social skills training packs. Some offenders should also be invited to devise ideas for a positive contribution to a community which would entail some form of social interaction.

5. Prison and probation volunteers should be harnessed to establish links with offenders at institutions in their area.

Dr Boswell lays much stress on the need to defeat, or at least diminish, the present discrimination against black offenders and women in community homes. She also offers one rather sensational speculation about the extent of physical and/or sexual abuse suffered by Section 53 offenders. She is convinced that at least 50 per cent of them have suffered in this way, but goes on to suggest that the real figure may be as high as 90 per cent. Of course, one is aware that there is all too much abuse of this kind, but I should be amazed if the true figure was anything like 90 per cent.

I should also point out that when I visited Feltham, the Section 53 offenders I met seemed a relatively happy lot.

VII Local Authority Secure Units

The cry goes up: keep young offenders out of penal custody! But in that case, what do you do with them instead? In the course of this book many answers are supplied to that question, and one which recurs repeatedly is to send them to local authority secure units. It seems right, therefore, to include a few facts about these. In this respect, I cannot do better than quote from a NACRO report of 1991:

Local authority secure accommodation is used for children and young people aged 10 and under 19 who are in the care of the local authority and whose behaviour is considered to represent a danger to themselves or to others. Secure units are also used for some young people who are in care on remand awaiting a court hearing.

In addition, some secure units accommodate young people who have been convicted of serious offences and are sentenced by a Crown Court under section 53 of the Children and Young Persons Act.

Most secure accommodation is the responsibility of local authority social services departments. Secure accommodation is also available at the two youth treatment centres run by the Department of Health, which offer around 70 specialized places not readily available elsewhere in the child care system. There are also some secure facilities available in health service establishments. Secure accommodation is not part of the prison system.

The size of units varies from two-place units up to 36-bedded establishments. However the majority of units are fairly small, with 23 establishments having less than eight beds.

I have visited several of these units, ranging from Aycliffe – world-famous and very large – to the little places with three inmates attached to local authority residential homes. There can, of course,

214

be no possible comparison between the provision in the two cases. NACRO continue:

There were 43 local authority secure units open at some point in the year ending 31 March 1989. The total number of places available on 31 March 1989 was 289. On 31 March 1988, there were 306 places available. This small decrease continues the trend of recent years. Since 1984 there has been a 20 per cent decline in the number of approved places in local authority secure units.

Secure accommodation is not evenly distributed around the country. For example, the North-East has 20 per cent of the total number of secure places in England, although only just over 6 per cent of the 10–17 year-olds in England live in that region. Similarly, the North-West has 14 per cent of the 10–17 population, yet 22 per cent of the secure beds. The West Midlands, on the other hand, has 11 per cent of the 10–17 year-old population but only 3 per cent of the total number of secure places in England. This imbalance in distribution of provision can result in some children and young people being placed a long way from their homes. In the year ending 31 March 1989, 22 per cent of those admitted to secure units were placed away from their home region.

It is clear that additional resources are necessary to provide a satisfactory framework of local authority secure accommodation. The amount, though considerable, would hardly be colossal, as neither the reformers nor the conservatives in this argument believe that more than a few hundred places for this category of offender will ever be needed. The trouble, however, is that at present some children and young people are placed a long way from their homes. We have seen elsewhere in this book the difficulties that can be caused by placing young offenders beyond easy reach of family and friends, and new accommodation would be necessary to put this right.

It is just as vital to ensure that the staff in these secure units are properly qualified. It can be argued, although this is controversial, that formal social work qualifications are not necessary for the majority of the staff in residential homes, most of whom are at the present time unqualified in this respect. However, as only the most difficult youngsters will ever need to be sent to local authority secure accommodation, they will require care and tuition of a high order if they are to be any better off than they are in prison.

In January 1993 the government announced in a written answer in the Commons that in England a further 60–65 places in local authority secure units are estimated to be needed to ensure that young offenders of 15 and 16 are not remanded to prison. At that time the government did not, however, say whether there were any plans to build more secure units to accommodate the greater numbers. They published at the same time the following statement of the secure accommodation available:

Secure accommodation by Region
31 December 1992

Regions and Locations	Managing Authorities	Number of Places
New Aycliffe Royston House	Durham	14 mixed
Aycliffe Community Home Special Unit	Durham	36 mixed
Netherton Park Elm Secure Unit	Northumberland	5 mixed
East Moor Community Home	Leeds	27 boys
Sutton Place Safe Centre	Humberside	5 mixed
Redsands Centre Oak House Unit	Cheshire	6 mixed
Redbank Community Home Vardy House	Lancashire	6 boys
Redbank Community Home Special Unit	Lancashire	26 boys
St Catherine's Community Home Laboure House	Nugent Care Society (St Helens)	5 girls
Briars Hey Community Home Orchard House	Lancashire	8 girls
Dyson Hall Community Home	Liverpool	8 boys
Park House Barton Moss Secure Unit	Salford	7 boys
St John's Safe Centre	Birmingham	8 mixed
Stoke House Sherbourne Unit	Coventry	8 mixed
Kesteven House	Lincoln	4 mixed
Derbyshire Children's Centre Greenacres Secure Unit	Derby	5 mixed
Amberdale Community Home	Nottinghamshire	8 mixed
Salters	Cambridgeshire	9 girls
Thornbury House	Oxon	3 boys
Middlesex Lodge Heathlands Unit	Hillingdon	9 girls
Little Heath Lodge	Newham	6 boys
Orchard Lodge	Southwark	8 boys
Frant Court Community Home	Greenwich	2 girls
Stamford House	Hammersmith	16 boys
Lansdowne Children's Centre	East Sussex	5 mixed
Beechfield	West Sussex	6 mixed
Fairfield	Hampshire	3 girls
Glen House Intensive Care Unit Medina Unit	Hampshire	8 mixed
Northbrook Community Home Atkinson Unit	Devon	12 mixed
Kingswood Secure Unit	Avon	20 boys

Source: Hansard

VIII *Joy-Riding*

My introduction to joy-riding came on a visit to the notorious Blackbird Leys Estate in Oxford in September 1992. A senior police officer took me round. During our time there we were passed by an insouciant young man in an expensive car who, the officer told me, was one of the ringleaders. We went on to discuss the difficulties of bringing such a young man to justice, particularly with regard to the right of silence.

On my next visit, I met another very impressive police officer even higher up the scale – a Chief Superintendent. In August 1991, he explained to me, he had produced a comprehensive memorandum entitled *Crime – Together We'll Crack It*. In his own words:

In the latest figures for car theft in Europe, the UK tops the league with 7.10 car thefts per 1,000 population ... in the Thames Valley police area, we can take little comfort from our position which shows us to be ahead of places like London in the number of car-related crimes. ... The car thief is 200 times more likely to be involved in an accident. Car crime has been described as a 'British disease'. They said that about football hooliganism as well. But what consolation is that to the innocent pedestrian, motorist or passenger laid up in hospital, or to the wife made a widow or to children made orphans because of the car thief's yearning for excitement and his utter disregard for the consequences of his actions. Such is reality.

The Chief Superintendent is well-versed in the research that has been conducted into this problem. He refers in particular to that undertaken by Jeff Briggs of the University of Durham. Briggs sees 'auto crime' as bolstering offenders' self-esteem and status. In his view, 'Joy-riders would seem to have a strong sense of identity which seems to be reinforced by their dealings with the judicial system.'

217

The Home Office endorses this view by saying that custodial sentences may not only fail in many cases to prevent further offending, but can indeed provide status and education in car crime.

Against that background, the Chief Superintendent framed three broad objectives which he and his colleagues are now endeavouring to pursue:

1. To ensure an effective and flexible police response to the problems of auto crime.

2. By working with others, to identify and implement a broad range of responses to the problems identified.

3. To ensure that the media, and through them the public, are aware of the nature and scale of the problem and the actions being taken on behalf of the community.

In his conversation with me, the Chief Superintendent made the claim in all modesty that considerable progress had been made since the craze first started, particularly in isolating the wrongdoers. He still maintained what the other officer had told me the year before – that the right of silence gave the young delinquent a great advantage in the face of interrogation when he was accompanied by a solicitor. Like other police chiefs – see the evidence earlier of the Chairman of the Police Federation – the Chief Superintendent would like to see the right modified to the point where it could at least be mentioned in court that the defendant had insisted on remaining silent. Again, like the Chairman of the Police Federation, he felt that the courts were very much inhibited in dealing with young offenders by not having anywhere to send the persistent offender. In his view, the so-called secure units of local authorities were frequently not secure.

I was much interested in what he told me about the strenuous efforts being made to bring understanding of crime in all its implications to local schools. What struck me most was the positive attempts being made to involve the whole community in the struggle against crime, particularly joy-riding. After seeing him, I moved on to visit the Oxford Probation Office where two ladies closely involved with this co-operative effort brought me thoroughly up to date. Not only the police and the Probation Service, but also business leaders and other respected citizens had joined together in a remarkable new venture called the Oxfordshire Motor Project Car Crime Programme (TRAX). In their own words:

TRAX is a company with charitable status. It has been set up and is managed by representatives from local business, the Magistrates, the Probation Service, Social Services, the Youth Service, the Police and Road

218

Safety. The project's aim is to channel the natural enthusiasm in young people for vehicles into exciting and legitimate activities. TRAX is a community-based project with workshop premises in Cowley, Oxford – it has primarily a crime prevention/diversion focus aimed at youngsters aged 14 and over who have not yet become caught up in the spiral of car crime, but also includes an intensive offence-focused programme for high-risk car offenders run in conjunction with Oxford Probation Service.

Each participant on the car crime programme will take part in three sessions per week of three hours each. It will last for eight weeks making, therefore, a total of 72 hours. The principal aims of the programme are these:

1. To challenge offending and examine patterns of offending and motivation.

2. A workshop session developing mechanical skills through working on vehicles. This culminates in racing at a local track.

3. A weekly employment and leisure session.

The programme is targeted at offenders involved in taking motor vehicles without permission and the new offence of aggravated taking of motor vehicles. In addition to the programme for offenders, the workshop will be used for mechanical tuition, educational programmes and the building and preparation of cars and motor cycles for the benefit of non-offender youth groups. These youngsters, I gather, considerably outnumber the offenders though they will not mix with them during working hours.

The whole concept filled me with enthusiasm, if only because for the first time in my experience (though Oxford is by no means the only example of such enterprise), the community seems to be mobilizing on behalf of young offenders and non-offenders alike. At the time of my visit the motor project had been in action for only a couple of months, so it was impossible to measure the effects. I wish it every success.

IX Conclusions

This book is the third of a trilogy. In 1991 I published *Punishment and the Punished* on adult offenders and in 1992 *Prisoner or Patient* which dealt with mentally disordered offenders. Now it is the turn of young offenders. In *Punishment and the Punished* (as in my short book *The Idea of Punishment* in 1961), I based myself on the classical elements in a just sentence: deterrence, reform, prevention (keeping offenders out of circulation) and retribution – that is to say, a fair relationship between the gravity of the offence and the severity of the punishment. I put in a strong plea for the addition of reparation. I insisted again and again that we send far too many people to prison.

In *Prisoner or Patient* I finished with two main demands: one was for a greater improvement in the diagnosis of patients who are mentally disordered, with a view in a number of cases to their transfer to mental hospitals, including special hospitals. The second was for a far-reaching improvement in the Prison Medical Service and the psychiatric care available in prisons. In each case I tried to imbue my whole approach with a Christian spirit.

This book is primarily concerned with the *treatment* of young offenders. But in fact it is impossible to draw a sharp line between treatment, cause and prevention. The evidence from intermediate treatment makes that particularly clear. There are in existence at the present time a wide variety of practical schemes to make offending less likely to be successful. But when we come to 'causes of crime' I am only too well aware that dogmatism is highly dangerous.

As mentioned earlier, I carried out with much expert assistance an inquiry into the causes of crime for the Nuffield Foundation in the 1950s. Many factors, we concluded, might increase the risk of offending. We only identified one of them – broken homes – as a major influence beyond question. Since then, as we all know, the number of broken homes has all too painfully increased. No doubt offending, adult and youthful, would be much diminished if the Christian message propounded by the Bishop of Lincoln, for example, were more widely accepted. More fidelity in marriage would mean fewer broken homes and in the end much less delinquency. Again, on the side of social policy, unemployment, bad housing, homelessness, inadequate income support and other weaknesses make it far more likely that young people, though not of course only young people, will go wrong.

Three issues of much relevance to our inquiry have been dealt with all too briefly in this book: alcohol and drug abuse, the sexual abuse of children and the impact of pornography on young minds.

Lord Mancroft is a young member of the House of Lords whom I particularly admire. He had the courage to tell the Lords and the general public of his former addiction to alcohol and drugs and how he overcame it. I cannot agree, however, with his suggestion that drugs now forbidden should be placed on the same legal footing as alcohol. There seems no likelihood of this happening in Britain. For my part I cannot forget my experience in the New Horizon Youth Centre for the young homeless. I shared a lavatory with a number of heroin addicts – 30 of them were dead within a year.

Esther Rantzen has done more than any individual to bring the whole question of child abuse before the public. She has also made it possible for children who are abused to make their complaints heard. She has her critics, like all innovative reformers. I am sure myself that she has done and is doing much good.

Mary Whitehouse has won a unique position in the consciousness of the nation. Thirty years ago an unknown schoolteacher, she set out to challenge the forces of pornography. She has built up an organization now of 165,000 members and is still fighting the battle with undiminished zeal. In her evidence to me, Mary reminded me of the case of a boy of 13 who was convicted of horrendous bullying of another boy of about his age. There was considerable outcry when the judge complained, wrongly as he afterwards admitted, that there was no adequate way of dealing with him. Mary Whitehouse pointed out in *The Times* that the real culprits were those in the media and elsewhere who had created the culture in which the young bully had grown up.

In 1971 and 1972 I was chairman of a large committee which thoroughly investigated pornography and produced a comprehensive report. It only included one chapter on violence. No doubt if we were writing that report today we would give violence a leading and perhaps *the* leading position. The connection between

221

violence and crime will be disputed until the end of time. I do not myself expect that statistical proof of a coercive nature will ever ben produced. But in the course of the public discussion recently, starting with the horrifying murder of a 2-year-old boy, Mary Whitehouse has come boldly forward yet again and argued quietly that a clear connection between pornography and violent crime has now been established to the satisfaction of any honest enquirer. It is gratifying to her old friends and admirers that after so much ridicule and abuse she is now being widely hailed as having been right all along.

It has generally been accepted in this country, as in others, that a more lenient sentencing policy should be applied to young offenders (however defined) than to adults. There is no classical statement of the principles that should be applied in their case. There has been an underlying feeling that they are less guilty than their seniors when they commit the same offence, and the younger they are the less the guilt. It has also been strongly argued that penal custody does more harm to young people before their character is formed, and that alternative methods would have more chance of directing them to a better life.

Whatever the theory, which has been official policy in Britain since the early years of this century, there has been a striking difference in the 1980s in the sentencing policy applied to over-21s and under-21s. To take the crudest indication: the population of adult prisons increased by 7,170 between 1980 and 1990, while the number of under-21s in penal custody went down from 10,500 to 6,400. Penal reformers, none more eloquently than Andrew Rutherford, have hailed this dramatic change with understandable delight, but it can only be attributed to deliberate government policy to a limited degree. As one who took part in many debates on penal policy during this decade, I cannot remember the government spokesmen taking credit for it. The main credit goes to the judges and magistrates, the social workers, including probation officers, and the penal reformers.

It is natural to ask what effect this liberal policy has had on the rate of young offending. I am told by experts that the statistics are as yet inconclusive. Nevertheless, the champions of reform are entitled to point to not a few figures which suit their case. The proportion of young offenders found guilty or cautioned for indictable offences fell from 54 per cent to 46 per cent between 1980 and 1990. The 1991 figures are similar. The Home Office has warned me against treating these as proof that the more liberal sentencing policy has led to a diminution of young offending, but perhaps I can speak further on this matter as a result of a visit I paid to the Conservative Conference at Brighton in October 1992.

Penal reformers like myself have been saying quite nice things about most of the Conservative Home Office Ministers over the years. But we have been treating them with a mixture of pity and something less than admiration, as being the creatures of their Party Conferences. In 1992, the *Catholic Herald* were kind enough to ask me to visit the Conference as their representative with special reference to the law and order debate. In fact it was a fairly tame affair. There were no hysterical demands for hanging and flogging, and I escaped unscathed. I asked a Conservative friend whether he thought I would be debagged; he replied, 'They will be so busy debagging each other, they won't have time for you!' That is how it turned out.

In the event the Home Secretary, Kenneth Clarke, made a speech that could have been delivered without protest to the Howard League for Penal Reform, apart from a few Conference witticisms. According to one quality newspaper he received a less enthusiastic reception than others during the week. From my point of view all credit to him. I must quote here a firm statement he made that there had been a reduction in the number of young offenders: 'You will be as surprised as I was to be told that the overall number of young offenders is happily declining.' A Home Office official was kind enough to reply to a subsequent enquiry of mine as follows: 'The number of known juvenile offenders found guilty or cautioned for indictable offences has fallen by 40 per cent from 176,000 in 1985 to 105,000 in 1991. (It would appear from this information that the Home Secretary was referring not to all young offenders but to juveniles.)

The Home Office official warned me that 'part of the fall has been due to demographic factors'. Even when that has been taken into account, there has still been a 30 per cent fall in the number found guilty or cautioned per hundred of population; from 3.6 in 1985 to 2.5 in 1991. 'These figures,' he told me, 'do not support any view whether juvenile crime itself is falling. We do not have an adequate measure of youth crime: this is because we do not know the ages of those who committed offences that were not cleared up.'

In a letter to me the Home Secretary lent his authority to a similar statement: 'The basic position is that you cannot adequately measure youth crime.' Nevertheless I am entitled to form my own opinion, having studied all the evidence available. I am entitled to draw the conclusion that the more lenient methods of sentencing young offenders have worked out better than the more severe ones applied to their seniors.

This points, in my view, to the conclusion that the more lenient methods of sentencing would be appropriate not only to young but also to adult offenders.

I had written the above when I received a document from the Prison Reform Trust which does not alter any of my views, but in the light of the Trust's splendid work it must at least be referred to. The Trust share my conclusions that juvenile crime has gone down in recent years and that this can be connected with a more enlightened sentencing policy. In my view, however, they avoid the troublesome question of what should be done with the few hundred persistent or serious young offenders who cannot simply be left at home. Widespread indignation has been created at the time of writing by the decision of a judge to place a 15-year-old rapist on a supervision order, requiring him also to pay £500 to give his victim a good holiday (the decision was later overturned and the offender incarcerated). The Prison Reform Trust seems to me to see the whole issue in black and white: prison custody on the one hand or on the other leave the young offender at home. I hope that no one who has got this far will see the issue so crudely as that.

Perhaps I can now turn to the general attitude of penal reformers towards young offenders. The penal reform case has been very effectively deployed in recent years by NACRO, the Howard League, the Penal Reform Trust and many active individuals. It is appropriate to quote something from the House of Lords' debate on Young Offenders which I initiated on 24 June 1992:

NACRO's clearest recommendation was as follows: 'The government should raise the minimum age at which a young person can be sentenced to detention in a penal institution from 15 to 16 years.' That would exclude 15-year-olds from penal institutions. Further, NACRO wished the possibility to be explored of keeping all young offenders under 18 out of penal custody. That would mean that 15, 16 and 17-year-olds would all be excluded from young offender institutions.

The Minister gave a stone-walling reply to this statement. The Criminal Justice Act of 1991, he told the House, coming into force in October 1992, would exclude 14-year-olds from penal custody. 'We must make sure,' said the Minister, 'that it is implemented successfully and as it is intended.' The pressure will continue unabated.

After so much contact with those possessed of highly relevant experience, I should be a poor creature if I had no suggestions to make as to where we go from here. I say at once that I side with those reformers who insist that 15, 16 and 17-year-olds should be excluded from penal custody as soon as possible. The numbers of 15 and 16-year-olds are not large. In 1989 there were 109 15-year-olds in penal custody and 246 16-year-olds. The number of 17-year-olds was much more substantial – 1,225. But, large or small, if one believes that penal custody is seriously damaging to these young people, and some would call them children, a patent social evil should be terminated.

That, however, would be the easier task before us, the negative part of it. No one would seriously suggest that we had done our duty to the young people concerned by throwing open the doors of the penal institutions and forgetting all about them. In other words, one comes back again and again, as I did throughout my interviews, to the question: What do you do with these young people, or more vitally *for* these young people, if you don't send them to penal custody?

By now the diligent reader will have been introduced to, and perhaps bewildered by, the number of alternatives to penal custody. The list below, which is not exhaustive, provides the main headings. The first three involve what can only be called custody, though not penal custody:

1. Youth treatment centres – like St Charles and Glenthorne.

2. Local government secure units.

3. Treatment in hospital under psychiatric and psychological care – for example, St Andrew's in Northampton.

4. Bail and probation hostels, which allow free movement of inmates during the day.

5. Intermediate treatment, with all the varieties that come under that title. The great majority of young people attending intermediate centres are not convicted delinquents. Some of them are, but the great majority are 'at risk'. Attendance varies from an appearance twice a week to full-time activities. There is much variation also in the length of time for which a young person is required by the court to attend a centre. Some centres are provided by local authorities, some by voluntary bodies.

6. Probation, with all its varieties of supervision, some of which have been described above.

7. Community Service Orders, requiring work on behalf of the community.

8. Fines.

9. Cautions.

At this point I should mention the word 'therapy', which is used in a great many different contexts, as will be realized by this point in the book. It may involve the application of professional skills. On the other hand, on the Albatross Wing at Feltham, it is provided by prison officers with no professional qualifications but a good measure of tender loving care.

The word in vogue today – and I go along with it – is 'self-esteem', but that phrase has its own pitfalls. In London's Streetwise Project for male prostitutes, for example, they pride themselves on increasing the self-esteem among young people who are tragically short of it. In Streetwise, however, they provide condoms to give their unhappy young clients some prospect of safety as they pursue their distressing trade. Different policies prevail and the attempted solutions vary. Here, I am only concerned to point out a few of the problems and the attempted solutions.

Therapy is a word of many meanings and so is community care, or treatment in the community. It can and usually does mean treatment outside penal custody, but it can also mean involving the community as a whole in the treatment recommended. I have described above the efforts made in Oxford, for example, but certainly not in Oxford alone, to mobilize the community outside the penal and welfare agencies in the effort to counter the joy-riding craze. More widely, I should at least mention the close collaboration which social workers and probation officers are endeavouring to establish in many places with the families of young offenders and of young people at risk.

Speaking as one who has studied a large number of such arrangements at first hand, however briefly, I must pay tribute in the clearest possible way to the dedication of those involved. One or two scandals there have been and no doubt there will be again. But what part of our national life is free from scandal?

Some attempt must now be made, however inadequately, to assess the scale of the effort required. Mr Willis of the Dartington Social Research Unit, a particularly well-informed student of the situation, has suggested that no more than 300 secure places would need to be provided for the most difficult young offenders who would otherwise, as now, be sent to penal custody. He argues that nationally they exist already, outside the penal system, though he feels that they are badly distributed at present. No doubt if we are talking of 15 and 16-year-olds, 300 places might be enough, but from the figure quoted earlier, something much more considerable is required for 17-year-olds, and of course if we move beyond that age the number mounts rapidly.

Why is it thought that local authority secure units will be more suitable for young offenders than adult prisons or young offender institutions like Feltham? The subject at this point becomes very intricate. At the present time, local authority secure units vary enormously. There are, for example, secure places for about 50 in a famous centre like Aycliffe, while there are only two or three in some units attached to residential homes. The accommodation is very badly distributed, with hardly anything available in the South of England. For example: the North-East has 20 per cent of the total number of secure places in England, although only just over 6 per cent of the 10–17 year-olds live in that region. Conversely the West Midlands has 11 per cent of the 10–17 year-old population but 3 per cent of the total number of secure places. This imbalance in distribution of provision can result in a considerable number of young people being placed a long way from their homes.

It is often argued by penal reformers that it would be much cheaper to give a young person a sentence that keeps him out of penal custody than one that leads him into such custody. That may be so, but it may be very much not so. At the St Charles Youth Treatment Centre in Brentwood, the cost is £100,000 a year per patient; at Aycliffe, it is £50,000 a year for most of the inmates and £75,000 a year for those in secure conditions. The explanation of these high figures is not hard to seek. At St Charles, there is a staff of 90 to deal with 30 patients; at Aycliffe, the ratio of staff to patients is roughly 2 to 1 and two-thirds of the staff have formal qualifications as educationalists, psychologists, nurses or social workers. In Albatross, the therapeutic unit at Feltham, on the other hand, the staff-to inmate ratio is the reverse: 20 young offenders are looked after by 8 prison officers, with some outside assistance. The officers do not possess formal qualifications but are selected for their experience and good judgement. Albatross is very successful in the circumstances.

In discussing how best to treat young offenders, it is impossible not to pay close attention to the staff ratios and the qualifications involved. No one supposes that the vast majority of young offenders require confinement and treatment on the level of St Charles or Aycliffe. But it is impossible, as I hope I have brought out by now, to provide real caring on the cheap.

Judge Stephen Tumim, Her Majesty's Chief Inspector of Prisons, is already renowned for his emphasis on training as the only real justification for incarceration. In his evidence to me for this book, he was as insistent on the need to train staff up to governor level as he was on the need to train the inmates. David Evans, the General Secretary of the Prison Officers' Association, has been quoted earlier as saying that he would like to see prison officers receive a two-year training, as do probation officers and social workers. The same arguments apply, I am convinced, to those who are called on to supervise young offenders in the community. Training is a word of many possible meanings, but its meaning would be incomplete without a moral and if possible spiritual element. Prisons are at least equipped with chaplains, but at the present time this is not true so far as I am aware of local authority secure units.

Finally, I lay great significance on the evidence given to me by Alan Eastwood, the Chairman of the Police Federation, and by senior police officers when I went to Oxford to hear about the joy-riding problem. In Oxford – as in most parts of the country – magistrates and indeed the town court are faced with a dilemma when confronted with a persistent young offender. They don't want to send him or her to penal custody, but at present no other secure accommodation is available. In the event they are helpless, and the persistent young offender comes to view the courts with contempt.

I turn to the attitude of the government. I quoted at the beginning of this book the proposals set out by the Home Secretary in his very important statement of 2 March 1993. As mentioned earlier, the most striking feature of the proposals was the suggested establishment of a small number of secure units for persistent young offenders aged 12, 13, 14 and 15. These proposals did not come as a great surprise to me.

I myself approach the issue through a series of questions:

1. Do you agree that a limited number of young offenders aged 12, 13, 14 and 15 should be removed from home and housed in some kind of secure unit, a) in the interests of society and b) in their own interests?

    The answer in my case is a qualified 'yes'. I am sure that the number of persistent young offenders we are talking about is very small. Two hundred is the figure mentioned in government circles. This may suffice, but we must bear in mind that if we are to remove all the youngest people from penal custody the number is likely to be greater. Be that as it may, a considerable number of those who need to be removed are already housed in secure units.

    In my view, when we remove a child – only boys seem to be contemplated – we are taking on a heavy responsibility for his welfare. We are under an obligation to do all in our power to provide him with a more healthy environment than the one from which he is removed. With many exceptions, we must assume that children are more loved by their parents or foster parents than they are in institutions, and somehow or other we must make this up to them. It might be argued that we do not apply this test to adult prisoners. It is, however, generally accepted that the responsibility of children for their conduct is much less than that of adults and the responsibility of the authorities much greater.

2. Which government department should ultimately be responsible for these new units, if established? The government, initially at any rate, seem to intend that the ultimate responsibility should rest with the Home Office. I am sure that this would be a grievous error. In the first

228

place the Home Office is inevitably connected with the penal approach to sentencing, and the approach in this case is supposed to be educational. It should also, in my view, be therapeutic where necessary. In the second place the existing network of secure units is provided in most cases by the local authorities and in two cases by the Department of Health, this department being ultimately responsible for all the units.

It would be ludicrous to have one lot of units provided by the Home Office and another lot for which the Department of Health would be responsible. An expert suggests to me that there could be merit in bringing together all the different establishments to which young offenders can be sent under the aegis of one agency. This would enable expertise and good practice to be spread throughout the relatively small number of units which look after young offenders in a way which is currently impossible. There remains the question of which government department should ultimately be responsible for such an agency. For me, the only answer is the Department of Health, but my expert friend is by no means certain that this is the answer.

3. Do the present secure units provide the basis for most of what is necessary? Only to a very limited extent. They vary dramatically in size from 2 to nearly 50, the latter at Aycliffe in a centre comprising 120 young people in all. They are scattered higgledy-piggledy over the country with a noticeably lean provision in the south of England. Their staff are mostly without formal qualifications, though two-thirds of the staff at Aycliffe have educational, social work or nursing qualifications. The two Department of Health units – St Charles and Glenthorne – also have well-qualified staff.

    It is high time to place the whole system on an organized national footing.

4. Two questions do not admit of altogether satisfactory answers. First, how are children to be kept in touch with their homes? With only a limited number of secure units of reasonable size, it is inevitable that most parents will have to travel some distance to see their children. Special arrangements should be made to assist them to do this and for the children, as they progress, to pay home visits.

    Second, is there a danger that persistent young offenders housed together will corrupt each other and leave custody worse than when they went in? There can be no perfect answer to this question. At Aycliffe there is considerable movement between secure units and the rest of the centre so that bad apples have less chance to spread their rot. Similar arrangements might be attempted elsewhere. In the end it will be up to the staff to help these young people emerge better than when they went in.

    The training and selection of staff is all-important. If training and selection are inadequate, the whole scheme may well do more harm than good. Aycliffe and St Charles provide examples of the kind of training and selection required. I pin my hopes on the emergence of

229

young social workers who will dedicate themselves to these most vulnerable children.

In my view there is therefore only one solution to the problem of persistent young offenders: to provide a coherent system of local authority secure units with trained staff under the direction of the Department of Health. Such units will not spring up of their own accord and the whole matter requires co-ordinated national guidance. I plead with vehemence for an official inquiry, with a view to producing a national plan worked out in collaboration with the local authorities.

While this book was in proof, I initiated a debate in the House of Lords. I asked the government in the light of their statement of 2 March 1993 what proposals they had in mind for the treatment of juvenile offenders.

I followed lines which will be familiar to readers of this book. I said that I did not expect, or even hope for, too definite an answer from Lord Ferrers, the Home Office Minister replying to the debate. For a long time I hoped that Lord Ferrers, a very accomplished parliamentarian, would live up to the old Irish saying, 'Mind you, I've said nothing'. He gave much evidence of an open mind and undertook that the unanimous criticisms of the government's proposals would be carefully studied.

Towards the end of his speech, however, he explained that while the Department of Health would play an important part in the new arrangements, 'the fact that all the youngsters in the new places will be persistent juvenile offenders – offenders who are serving a sentence of the court – makes it eminently sensible for the Home Office to be primarily responsible for them'. None of the other speakers would have agreed with him for a moment. One can only hope that the government will do a U-turn on this as on more than one other issue.

Much of the evidence in this book indicates that a more enlightened sentencing policy has been applied to young offenders in recent years. The same, however, cannot be said of government policy towards their treatment in young offender institutions. Those sent to these places are not necessarily treated better than they would be in an adult prison.

I have visited Feltham on a number of occasions, also Aylesbury, and what I have said earlier about Feltham applies, to the best of my belief, to them all. The latest report (April 1991 to March 1992) from HM Inspector of Prisons paints a grim picture of life in Feltham: grim in the general plan of the establishment, grim in the size of its catchment area, so that many inmates are far from their

230

families, and especially grim in the way that the vulnerable and unsophisticated are thrown together with hardened young offenders from the inner cities. The result – bullying and suicide – has been tragic.

Feltham presents a supreme challenge, not only to those in power but to all those with a social conscience. The Governor of Feltham, Joe Whitty, is a man of exceptional idealism and courage. Some of his bold experiments have been described in these pages. It will be noted, however, that Father Gerald Ennis, who was the Catholic Chaplain at Feltham for three years, considers that the life lived by the young people there is less fruitful than it was a few years ago; today, there are fewer activities and inmates may find themselves confined to their cells for all but an hour or two a day. Governor Whitty has put the problem in the clearest possible way: unless he has more staff, he cannot begin to give effect to the rehabilitative policies which the government proclaims so proudly. It was gratifying that in the Lords' debate on young offenders on 24 June 1992, the Minister paid a considered tribute to the imaginative use that the Governor was making of his existing staff. Nice words, sincerely meant – but completely useless without a public commitment to more staff and better training.

The most obvious practical recommendations that I submit as a result of this study are therefore:

1. No young person should be sent to penal custody under the age of 16 immediately and 18 as soon as possible.

2. Some secure alternative to penal custody is clearly essential for grave or persistent offenders. A national plan is indispensable to work out arrangements of an educational and therapeutic character. The main responsibility for these arrangements should fall on the Department of Health, though close consultation with the Home Office and Department of Education will be necessary. Whatever form the new units take, the staff should be fully qualified, no doubt in a number of different ways.

3. Intermediate treatment, in the broadest sense, and supervision through the Probation Service should be assisted with much more government finance.

4. A large increase in the staffing of young offender institutions is indispensable if existing declarations of policy are to be a reality.

Whether these essential improvements are effected in the short or long run will depend on public attitudes and above all on government leadership.

However, I would not like readers of this book to conclude that

231

no large achievements are possible in this field without government assistance. On 2 November 1992, I attended two functions which helped to prove the opposite.

In the morning, I attended a conference at Pentonville Prison to discuss the work of the Young Offenders' Group of the Prince's Trust. There were present nearly 200 men and women concerned with young offenders in one way or another. Prince Charles himself and the Home Secretary, Kenneth Clarke, spoke firmly in support of the Young Offenders' Group which, we were told, had handed out £450,000 to some 100 projects. The money had been given from Prince Charles's own fund-raising exertions. One point made by Prince Charles came home to me with special force. 'Young offenders,' he said, 'should be made to compensate the victims of their crimes by doing more work in the community.' As one who introduced the first Private Member's Bill in the House of Lords on behalf of victims, I responded whole-heartedly to that message. The Prince concluded by saying, 'Given a sense of belonging, young people could work creatively through the community rather than reacting negatively and sometimes primitively against what must appear to be an unsympathetic world.'

In the evening, I attended the first Annual General Meeting of the Friends of Feltham Young Offenders' Institution. We were addressed – one might say with unique authority – by Jimmy Boyle, whom I last met in the Barlinnie Special Unit, Glasgow. Since then, he has done social work of the utmost value and written memorably. He had earlier been described as the most dangerous man in Scotland.

The message which emerged alike from Prince Charles and Jimmy Boyle, whose life experiences have been utterly different, was the same: There is no limit to the help that can be given by ordinary citizens to young offenders, enabling them to believe in themselves for the first time and to achieve personal fulfilment.

When I was finishing this book, I received a copy of *Living Dangerously – Young Offenders in their Own Words* by Roger Graef, who impressed me greatly when I interviewed him for my book *Prisoner or Patient*. No one interested in young offenders should fail to read *Living Dangerously*, which I have studied with much benefit. A few sentences must be quoted here:

We judge these young offenders as if they have the same opportunities, protection and values and had somehow turned their backs on them and us. We call them evil and try 'to teach them a lesson', as if we were all playing the same game on a level playing field and they had cheated. Perhaps we have cheated them.

232

Graef dwells on many of the poignant themes in the lives of young offenders which have been emphasized throughout this book. He refers to the possibility of their becoming useful, law-abiding citizens and concludes:

Not all the people in this book will make that transition. But after watching them closely, I feel that all of them could, given will-power and resource-fulness on their part and encouragement, tolerance and opportunity on the part of those they meet along the way. The challenge is theirs, but the consequences if they succeed or fail are chiefly ours. They are, after all, our children.

In the end, I come back to the Christian Gospel. We all remember the parable of the sheep and the goats in Matthew XXV. Jesus is depicted as saying: 'I was in prison and you came to me. Insomuch as you did it to the least of my brethren, you did it to me.' That message has been applied in practice over the years by so many Christians and non-Christians, who give their lives to serving those who have fallen into error or crime, whether in custody or otherwise under the care of the State.

Some words came back to me which reflect their spirit and, however feebly, my own:

> Then, with a rush, the intolerable craving
> Shivers throughout him like a trumpet call:
> Oh! to save these, to perish for their saving,
> Die for their life, be offered for them all.

Index